THE CRIME BUFF'S GUIDE TO

OUTLAW NEW MEXICO

RON FRANSCELL

angel fire press

San Antonio, Texas

angel fire press

All photos by Ron Franscell unless otherwise noted.

Library of Congress Cataloging-in-Publication data is available on file.
Franscell, Ron, 1957-
ISBN-10: 0692026819 (pbk)
ISBN-13: 978-0-692-02681-6 (pbk)

Printed in the United States of America
10 9 8 7 6 5 4 3 2 1

To Owen
Who will make his own history

"The whole course of human history
may depend on a change of heart in one
solitary and even humble individual—
for it is in the solitary mind and soul of
the individual that the battle between
good and evil is waged and
ultimately won or lost."

—M. Scott Peck

OLD WEST AND NEW WEST
An introduction

No place illustrates the collision of the Old and New West like the American Southwest. The settlement, the battles, the politics and, yes, the crime in New Mexico exemplify very starkly the growing pains of an ambitious, adventurous nation.

New Mexico is in the "Deep Southwest," a desiccated mirror image of Dixie with deserts instead of bayous, heat without humidity, different cultures in conflict. And like the South, the line between history and mythology is razor thin.

The Southwest's crime history, especially from the outlaw period, often erases the line altogether. And we might never disentangle fact from fiction. But myth is a real part of the Wild West, and without it, history might be less than the sum of its parts.

This book will transport you to the scene of one of the bloodiest prison riots in American history, the spot where Bonnie and Clyde were almost captured, and the exact location of a post-war UFO hoax that bilked ordinary people out of their savings. With its companion volume, OUTLAW ARIZONA, this book points the way to spots where infamous crime figures—John Dillinger, Doc Holliday, Billy the Kid, Bonnie & Clyde, and Wyatt Earp, among others—once stood. It will take you to the many places in our Wildest West where ordinarily law-abiding people finally grew frustrated with the pace of justice and took the law into their own hands.

Let this book be your window. Our appreciation of history begins in the places where it happened. And now the magic of Global Positioning Satellites (GPS) allows you to stand in a precise historic spot, as best as our modern technology and imaginations can muster. We have made every attempt to put you literally within inches of the past.

The Old West was many things, not the least of which is a wild history of crime, punishment, survival, and redemption. Our New West is many other things—but remains a place where crime is a salient part of history.

History is how we know, how we learn. And being there makes all the difference.

—**Ron Franscell**

How to use this book

The entries in this book are divided into two chapters, one about New Mexico in general and one about Billy the Kid. Each entry has physical and GPS directions that will let you stand in the footsteps of history–not in the general vicinity, but literally on a spot relevant to one of the Southwest's most notable and infamous crimes or figures.

Crimes big and small have been committed every single day since mankind began to distinguish right from wrong. This book cannot begin to aggregate every injustice, every crime, every inhumanity ever visited upon New Mexico, although even the smallest crime certainly affects victims, survivors, and communities as much as the most celebrated crimes in our history. And in some cases here, we have chosen only a few representative sites. So please don't be offended if you feel we've overlooked a crime or site you believe should have been included.

A word of warning: Many of these sites are on private property. Always seek permission before venturing onto private land. Do not trespass. It's rude, illegal, and almost everybody in the Southwest has a gun.

We made every effort to be precise in our facts and directions, but being human we might have erred. If you believe we should include a certain crime in future editions—or if you see an error that should be corrected—please send a note to Ron Franscell c/o Angel Fire Press, 25270 Flaming Arrow, San Antonio TX 78258.

A note about GPS accuracy

GPS readings are affected by many things, including satellite positions, noise in the radio signal, weather, natural barriers to the signal, and variations between devices.

Noise—static, interference, your car roof, or competing frequencies—can cause errors up to 30 feet. Clouds, bad weather, mountains, or buildings can also skew readings up to 100 feet.

While we've tried to make every GPS coordinate in all our Crime Buff's Guides as precise as possible, we can't be sure you'll visit under the same conditions. The best possible way to get an accurate reading is to be sure the satellites and your receiver have a clear view of each other, with no clouds, trees, or other interference. If your device doesn't bring you to the right spot, look around. It's likely within a few paces.

NEW MEXICO

WEST MESA SERIAL KILLER
Albuquerque
The serial killer's makeshift grave sites were near Dennis Chavez Boulevard SW and 118th Street SW, in the area of GPS 35.03556, -106.753056.

On a brisk February morning in 2009, a woman walking her dog spied a large bone sticking up through the dirt. It didn't look like any animal bone she'd seen before.

Albuquerque police investigated and determined it was a human femur. Within weeks, investigators had unearthed the skeletons of eleven women and one unborn child, all young, all buried in shallow graves, and all reported missing between 2003 and 2005. Ten were known prostitutes or drug addicts; one simply disappeared on her way to a local park.

The burial site covered several acres and despite the wealth of bones, there was little other forensic evidence.

Theories abound.

Police suspected a violent thug named Lorenzo Montoya, who tied up and strangled a hooker in his trailer near West Mesa. Her protective pimp killed Montoya that night. Reports of missing women dropped off drastically after that.

They also looked hard at a pimp named Fred Reynolds, who knew at least one of the murder victims and kept

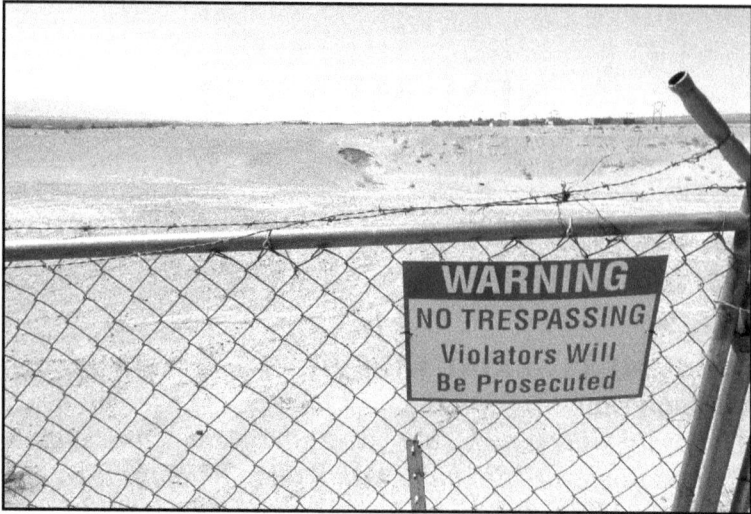

Vacant subdivision on Albuquerque's West Mesa where the serial killer's victims were buried.

photos of missing women. He died of natural causes in 2009.

In 2010, FBI agents and Albuquerque cops searched two homes and a business owned by a health-food vendor and travel photographer from Joplin, Missouri, who frequently attended the New Mexico State Fair. No charges were ever filed and the case remains unsolved.

A $100,000 reward has been offered and an Albuquerque Police Department website harvests tips about the West Mesa killer. See *www.helpuscatchakiller.com.*

DESPERATE FOR A BABY
Albuquerque
The crime scene is on Cibola National Forest Road 242 almost twenty miles east of Albuquerque, at GPS 35.034541, -106.355233. This site is remote and on private property.

The afternoon of July 7, 1987, was insufferably muggy in Albuquerque, especially for nineteen-year-old Darci Pierce, who was nine months pregnant. In fact, she was overdue. In just a few hours, she would meet her husband at the hospital, where labor would be induced and their child would be born.

Darci's family had suffered through the past couple years with her. Darci desperately wanted to be a mother and had finally gotten pregnant again after a miscarriage. Now she was about to have a baby and everyone was waiting for that happy phone call. Just a few more hours.

She pulled her dusty Volkswagen Beetle into the parking lot of the pre-natal clinic at Kirtland Air Force Base (5400 Gibson Boulevard SE, at GPS 35.05807, -106.581284), and parked beside a Blazer, where another pregnant mother, Cindy Ray, was about to go inside for her last doctor visit before she gave birth in the next two weeks.

Motherhood had brought them together.

Problem was, Darci Pierce wasn't expecting at all. She'd faked her lengthy pregnancy, which followed her fake miscarriage. For almost two years, she wore maternity clothes and bought all the books. She converted a spare bedroom into a nursery. She talked about her baby all the time. She even kept a packed suitcase in the hall closet for the big trip to the hospital.

But now her lie would be exposed if she didn't have a real baby. And she came to the Kirtland clinic to find one.

Later that night, a blood-splattered Darci Pierce stumbled into a hospital emergency room, carrying a newborn baby. She told nurses she had just given birth in her car. But something wasn't right. Darci only wanted a birth certificate for the child she had already named Amanda Michelle. When Darci refused ordinary care for herself and her baby, doctors called police.

Under questioning, the whole horrid story spilled out.

Darci kidnapped Cindy Ray from the clinic parking lot and drove her into the Cibola National Forest east of the city. There, beside a seldom traveled dirt road, she strangled Ray and carved her living fetus from her womb using only a set of car keys.

Her grisly Caesarean surgery had been interrupted by a passerby who stopped to investigate the Volkswagen parked in the middle of the narrow road, its doors still open. "My friend and I need to be left alone," Darci hollered at him several times. He assumed she was with a man—at least until he saw a woman lying in the brush, her dress hiked up over her waist—and that they were having sex.

In 1988, Pierce was convicted of first-degree murder, kidnapping and child abuse. She is serving a life sentence, but is eligible for parole in 2018.

Cindy Ray (1964-1987) was buried in the City Cemetery in Payson, Utah. Her grave is in Block 45, Lot 30 (GPS 40.051399, -111.719591).

Ray's baby girl survived and was raised by her father. She now lives in Utah.

ABDUCTION OF INNOCENCE
Albuquerque
The former Canyon Motel, now gone, was at 13001 East Central Avenue, or GPS 35.069043, -106.503193.

Decades after she died, Linda Lee Daniels' name still haunts Albuquerque. In 1986, her random abduction, horrific rape, and pitiless murder stunned the city and lodged in the memory like no other modern crime.

Twenty-two-year-old Daniels was a junior anthropology major at the University of New Mexico. Around 7 p.m. on January 12, she picked up some groceries at a supermarket so she could fix Sunday dinner for her fiancé at his family's home on Robert Dale Drive NE in the city's middle-class Northeast Heights.

But when she never arrived, her fiancé found her Mustang parked in front of his house, the driver's door ajar, and groceries scattered from the driveway to the front porch.

Daniels had been abducted by three men who'd missed their chance to snatch her from the supermarket, so they followed her home.

For five days, Albuquerque was in a panic and police had few leads. But they caught a break when they published a murky ATM photo of a man withdrawing money with Daniels' card the night she disappeared. A tip led cops to a bar where one of the men had been seen and where Daniels' credit card was found in a bathroom trash bin. The man in the ATM photo was identified as a teenager named James Scartaccini.

Police soon arrested Scartaccini and two friends, Wallace Pierce and Sidney Sliger. And they quickly implicated a greasy, scrawny ex-convict named Johnny Zinn.

Zinn, who'd served time for armed robbery and bragged about connections to shadowy porn figures, had offered the three men $1,500 to bring him a woman for a porn film. The hapless trio couldn't even convince hookers to do it, so they hatched a plot to kidnap an unwilling victim.

They stalked parking lots and supermarkets for days but came up empty.

Then they saw the pretty, petite, and blond Linda Lee Daniels in a grocery checkout line and followed her home.

They took her to the seedy Canyon Motel, where Zinn waited for them. They stripped her naked and injected her with sedatives to prevent her from screaming or escaping.

All night, the four men took turns raping the blindfolded Daniels at knifepoint.

The next day, Zinn dispatched his young henchmen to take Daniels to Farmington, where a porn movie crew supposedly was waiting for them. But along the way, Zinn changed the plan: He ordered them to kill Daniels.

The three men took her into the Jemez Mountains on New Mexico 126. They stopped on a narrow bridge (GPS 35.908970, -106.712386) near the Seven Springs Fish Hatchery and dragged Daniels down to a snow bank under the road, where they shot her in the back of the head with a .22-caliber pistol as she begged for mercy.

A week after Daniels' slaying, Scartaccini led cops to her body. Nine months later, a Las Cruces jury convicted the murderous mastermind Zinn of first-degree murder, rape, kidnapping and sixteen other charges. He was sentenced to life plus ninety-six years in prison.

The remote forest bridge where co-ed Linda Lee Daniels' body was dumped by her killers in 1986.

Wallace Randolph Pierce, the shooter, pleaded guilty to first-degree murder and three other counts, and was sentenced to life plus thirty-six years.

James Scartaccini, who was only seventeen at the time, testified against the others for immunity. In 1990, facing allegations that he was beating his teenage wife, he hanged himself.

Sidney Sliger also got immunity for testifying against the others. He served only three years in prison for the rape, and is now a free man.

Linda Lee Daniels (1965-1986) was buried in the Olinger Highland Cemetery in Thornton, Colorado.

BAD BLOOD
Albuquerque
Sunset Memorial Park is at 924 Menaul Boulevard NE. The youngest victims' graves are at Block 6, Section 66, or GPS 35.10832, -106.63516.

In 1981, Susie Newsom and Tom Lynch divorced in New Mexico. The split was openly hostile, and the custody battle for their two young sons was venomous.

Susie snatched her boys and moved back to her native North Carolina, where she soon started a new romance with her cousin, Dr. Fritz Klenner. Klenner practiced medicine (although he never actually went to college), was a Klan supporter and obsessive gun nut, and even in the 1980s, required black patients to sit in a separate waiting room.

Then in July 1984, Tom Lynch's mother and sister were murdered in broad daylight after coming home from church in Oldham, Kentucky. Local police had no motive and no suspects.

Less than a year later, Susie Newsom's own father, mother and grandmother were massacred in their North

Carolina home. This time, though, police had a hunch about the killer: Susie Newsom's parents had endorsed giving custody of their two grandsons to Tom Lynch, not their daughter.

The more police learned about Susie Newsom and Fritz Klenner, the more convinced they became that they were involved in the five murders. An arrest was imminent.

On June 3, 1985, police spotted Newsom and Klenner in his Chevy Blazer and followed him, not knowing Newsom's two sons, Jim and John, were in the backseat. Suddenly, Fritz started shooting out his window as he led them on a high-speed chase.

Before they could stop Klenner, he detonated a bomb in the SUV, killing himself, Susie and the boys. An autopsy found Susie's sons had already been poisoned with cyanide before the explosion, and perhaps because the poison wasn't acting fast enough, they had both been shot in the head, too.

Susie Newsom (1946-1985) was buried in Greensboro, North Carolina. Fritz Klenner (1952-1985) was buried in nearby Reidsville.

James and John Lynch were brought home to Albuquerque and buried together in Sunset Memorial Park.

The sordid story has been told in Jerry Bledsoe's 1988 book, *Bitter Blood*, and was made into a 1995 TV movie of the same title, starring Harry Hamlin and Kelly McGillis.

JUSTICE DELAYED
Near Albuquerque
The crime scene was about 15 miles west of Albuquerque on the side of Interstate 40's eastbound lanes. It has been covered by road expansion.

Late on November 8, 1971, Trooper Robert Rosenbloom was just a week away from a promotion in the New Mexico State Police when he stopped three black men in a green Ford sedan on the interstate. For the six-year veteran, it was like a hundred other stops he'd made.

But it wasn't. Rosenbloom was gunned down after finding guns in the trunk, and the Ford sped away. The twenty-eight-year-old father of two, shot in the chest and throat, died alone on a dark roadside.

Trooper Rosenbloom

A massive manhunt was launched for Ralph Goodwin, Michael Finney and Charlie Hill, all members of a violent black-separatist movement called the Republic of Africa who'd been on their way to Jackson, Mississippi, to start a race war. Hiding out in Albuquerque, they eluded police for almost two weeks before they sneaked aboard TWA Flight 106 at the local airport. Once airborne, they hijacked the plane to Cuba.

Cuban police briefly detained the three terrorists, then released them with all the questionable privileges of Cuban citizens.

Goodwin drowned at a Havana beach in 1975. Finney died of throat cancer in 2005, also in Cuba. Hill remains in exile with no intentions of returning to the US except "in a coffin."

In 2001, the New Mexico State Police renamed its Albuquerque office the Robert Rosenbloom Building (2501 Carlisle Boulevard NE, at GPS 35.108211, -106.604551).

Rosenbloom is buried in the Good Shepherd section of Las Cruces' Hillcrest Cemetery, at GPS 32.30240, -106.85305).

THE WITNESS-PROTECTION KILLER
Albuquerque

The murder scene was at the North Court Trailer Park, 10014 Second Street NW (Space 14), or GPS 35.195069, -106.611467. This is private property.

In 1979, Marion Albert Pruett was serving time in an Atlanta prison for armed robbery when he snitched about his cellmate's stabbing by a mobster inmate. It proved to be Pruett's Get Out of Jail Free card: He was placed in the federal witness protection program, given $800 a month, a trailer in New Mexico, and a new name—Charles "Sonny" Pearson.

In April 1981, Pruett walked into an Albuquerque police station and reported that somebody had killed his common-law wife Pamela Barker (aka Michelle Pearson) and burned her corpse. He led cops to her charred corpse in the desert (at about 17th Avenue SW and Jardine Road in an undeveloped area known as Unit Nine, or GPS 35.228470, -106.738430).

Investigators found Pamela's skull had been smashed with a ball-peen hammer. She was identified only by the serial number on her Medic-Alert bracelet.

But by the time police had a name, Pruett was long gone. But he wasn't done killing.

In September, Pruett robbed a bank in Jackson, Mississippi, taking loan officer Peggy Lowe as a hostage. He later shot her in the back of the head.

The following Sunday, Pruett arrived in Fort Smith, Arkansas, looking for someplace to rob. Since the banks were closed, he parked in a secluded area where he snorted cocaine and gulped whiskey before robbing and kidnapping convenience store clerk Bobbie Jean Robertson, whom he shot to death after stealing $165.

Four days later, Pruett walked into two different Colorado convenience stores and fatally shot two clerks.

After he was arrested and awaiting trial in Mississippi, Pruett happily gave interviews to local reporters in which he admitted his crimes and dubbed himself "The Mad Dog Killer."

He was eventually convicted in all the killings in four states, and sentenced to die by an Arkansas jury. He blamed his robbery and killing spree on a $4,000-a-week cocaine habit.

While on death row, he continued to puff up his own legend, offering to reveal another murder victim's body if he could be on *Geraldo*. And Pruett had another surprise: He confessed to killing his own cellmate, whose 1979 stabbing Pruett had falsely blamed on a mobster so he could get out of prison.

After killing at least five people while in the witness protection program, Pruett was executed by lethal injection in 1999.

GUILTY UNTIL PROVEN INNOCENT
Albuquerque
The murder scene—undeveloped desert at the time—is now amid subdivisions near Four Hills Road SE, at GPS 35.060374, -106.490265.

On a chilly February morning in 1974, a crow hunter in the Manzano foothills east of the city stumbled upon a grisly scene: A young man's mutilated corpse half-buried beneath a sagebrush, his pants yanked down around his knees.

William Velten, a 26-year-old student and Vietnam veteran, had been shot four times in the mouth and his chest slashed with a big knife. He'd also been castrated and his severed penis stuffed in his mouth.

The military veteran Velten (1948-1974) was buried in Section X, Site 252 of the Santa Fe National Cemetery, at GPS 35.697894, -105.948753.

Four Los Angeles bikers, all members of the reputedly violent Vagos motorcycle gang, were passing through Albuquerque at the time. A motel maid later told police she witnessed Velten's murder by the four men, and they were arrested. Ron Keine, Thomas Gladish, Richard Greer, and Clarence Smith were convicted and sentenced to die.

Six months later, the maid recanted, but the judge refused a new trial.

Meanwhile, the four bikers were locked 24 hours a day in their 6-by-9 cells on Death Row, allowed only one shower a week and an hour of exercise alone in a small cage.

Then a miracle.

In the fall of 1975, a former cop named Kerry Lee found Jesus and confessed to Velten's murder to his pastor and police. At first, prosecutors didn't believe him—even though he described the slaying in gruesome detail and drew an accurate map of the crime scene. At the time, Lee was shrugged off as a nut case and no charges were filed.

The bikers remained on Death Row for two years, despite Lee's confession. When a judge finally freed them, one of the bikers was just nine days away from his first date with New Mexico's gas chamber. They walked away as free men in 1976.

At his 1978 trial, Lee told his sordid story: After meeting the homosexual Velten in a bar, where they drank and took some drugs, Lee and Velten drove into the nearby desert. After their car got high-centered, Lee claims he flew into a rage when Velten made sexual overtures. He shot and emasculated Velten, then concealed the body in sagebrush near an arroyo and threw his handgun into the darkness. He later returned with a girlfriend to move the corpse.

A couple months after the murder, a boy riding his bike through the arroyo had found the gun, which was later linked to Lee.

Lee was convicted and sentenced to a maximum 55 years in prison, but served only eight years. Paroled in 1986, he moved to Florida.

However, his religious conversion apparently didn't stick. In 1987, he killed another man. A jury convicted him of manslaughter and he was paroled in 2000. In 2002, he went to federal prison for possessing a handgun. He has since been released.

DEATH AT THE OFFICE
Albuquerque
Emcore is at 10420 Research Road, or GPS 35.055022, -106.531509. This is private property.

Robert Reza and Adrienne Basciano had lived together for years and had twin sons. They had even worked side-by-side for several years at Emcore, a fiber optics and photovoltaic products factory in southeast Albuquerque.

But when their relationship turned violent, Basciano wanted out … and Reza didn't. An agonizing custody battle erupted. Frustrated and enraged, Reza's fury finally boiled out in a rambling, forty-page manifesto and a deadly plan.

On the morning of July 12, 2010, Reza went to Emcore armed with a 45-caliber semi-automatic handgun.

He first shot one worker dead on the steps outside Emcore, then searched for Basciano inside. He found her sitting at a picnic table with Michele "Scrappy" Turner. He shot Basciano several times, then ran down Turner and killed her.

Reza then entered another building, wounding three other workers before he retreated to an office and shot himself.

Basciano lost a lung but survived the deadliest office shooting in New Mexico's history.

Turner was buried in Albuquerque's Sunset Memorial Park, 924 Menaul Boulevard NE. Her cremains are in the Times and Seasons Room, Niche 84, Level B (GPS 35.106503, -106.633393). The whereabouts of victim Sharon Cunningham's remains are private.

A year later, Emcore unveiled a memorial garden to the victims on its campus.

SHERIFF PERFECTO ARMIJO
Albuquerque

Mount Calvary Cemetery is at 900 Edith Boulevard NE. This grave is in the northeastern corner of the Santa Barbara section at GPS 35.10032, -106.63689.

Perfecto Armijo (1845-1913) was the consummate lawman, and a native son of the territory. While he's not well-known to history, he was renowned in his day, when a lot of lawmen tended to be as bad as they were good.

Not Sheriff Armijo.

In February 1883, Armijo had jailed a killer named Milt Yarberry, a former town marshal who was convicted and waiting to hang. Word came that a mob of vigilantes had gathered to break into the jail and lynch Yarberry.

Armijo didn't wait. He strode alone into the angry crowd and spoke directly to the ringleaders, convincing them to abandon their murderous plot and be patient with justice.

A few months later, Armijo supervised Yarberry's legal hanging on the county gallows in Old Town.

Yarberry was buried with the noose still around his neck in Mount Calvary Cemetery, not far from where Armijo himself would be buried thirty years later. Today, Yarberry's grave marker is missing.

A MURDEROUS MOLESTER
Artesia
Dena Lynn Gore was abducted in Artesia and her body found on the remote Squaw Canyon Ranch sixty miles north of Artesia. She is buried in the Cedarvale Cemetery in the ghost town of White Oaks, about 100 miles northwest of Artesia. Her grave is at GPS 33.74109, -105.74647.

Dena Lynn Gore was only nine, but she was already a feisty tomboy. She preferred baseball to dolls, loved jeans more than dresses.

On the afternoon of July 17, 1986, she borrowed her older brother's bike for a six-block trip to an Allsup's convenience store to buy a soda pop. She vanished.

Five days later, her naked body, trussed up and badly decomposed, was found partially buried on the Squaw Canyon Ranch, sixty miles north of Artesia. She'd been found by Steve Clark, the ranch manager—who suspected his younger brother Terry Clark was involved in the girl's disappearance. At the time, Terry Clark was out of

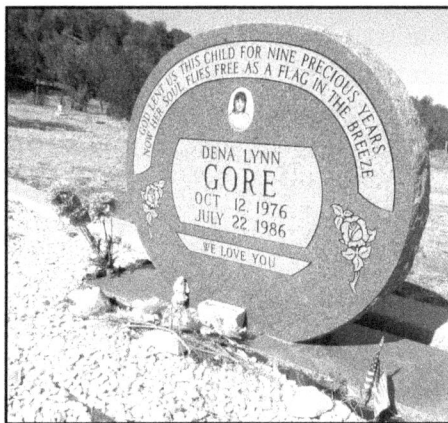

Dena Lynn Gore's grave

15

prison while appealing his conviction in a 1984 child rape, and he was living on the ranch, too.

His older brother was right.

Clark was arrested and while in jail, he admitted to a minister that he killed Dena Lynn Gore. Five months later, he pleaded guilty to kidnapping and murder. During the penalty phase, Clark admitted that he killed Dena when she threatened to tell on him. Rather than be arrested, he shot her three times in the back of the head. Under New Mexico law, the death penalty is warranted if a witness to a crime is murdered.

But in 1996 the state Supreme Court overturned his death sentence because, it said, Clark's legal rights had been violated. A second jury subsequently condemned Clark again.

In 1988, New Mexico enacted the "Dena Lynn Gore Law" to prevent certain convicted criminals, such as rapists or molesters, from being free on bail while they appeal.

On November 6, 2001, Terry Clark was led to the New Mexico death chamber. His 1984 victim was among the witnesses at Clark's execution by lethal injection. He was the first New Mexico inmate to die in more than forty years, and the last before the state outlawed capital punishment in 2009. The whereabouts of his remains are unknown.

But Clark left one more mystery with his cryptic last words: "Fifteen minutes." The reference likely came from Sister Helen Prejean's 1993 book, *Dead Man Walking*, which suggested it would take fifteen minutes for a dead man's soul to reach Heaven.

Or Hell.

See also "New Mexico Death Chamber" (Santa Fe)

THE AZTEC UFO
Aztec

The alleged alien crash site is about ten miles northeast of Aztec on Road 2770, at GPS 36.87767, -107.84133. It's remote, accessible only by a dirt road and a short hike.

In 1948, just one year after a strange alien ship crashed near Roswell, another extraterrestrial craft plunged to earth near the little town of Aztec, New Mexico.

The metallic disc's hull was seamless and measured almost a hundred feet across. It also contained sixteen humanoid bodies, all about three feet tall. As in Roswell, the military surreptitiously cleaned up the crash scene in Hart Canyon and hauled the wreckage—and the slightly charred alien corpses—to a top secret facility to be studied.

But the government couldn't keep its secret very long. In 1950, *Variety* columnist Frank Scully wrote a book, *Behind the Flying Saucers*, in which he spilled all the secrets of Aztec and Roswell. In a startling revelation, he revealed how the aliens' spacecraft technology had given birth to a new device that could find oil and natural reserves miles below ground.

And that magical device, invented by a mysterious government geomagnetism expert named Dr. Gee, was sold to oil-exploration executive Silas Newton, who was now seeking investors. For just $18,500, Newton would even sell one of the extraordinary machines to anyone who had the cash.

Denver millionaire Herman Flader and other investors flocked to Newton. Flader alone gave $231,000 and Newton harvested hundreds of thousands more from other eager backers.

One problem: It was all a hoax.

Con-man Newton and an Arizona radio-parts salesman named Leo GeBauer (aka "Dr. Gee") had contrived the scheme. They fooled a nationally known journalist into giving them credibility, and then they just cashed the checks. That $18,500 machine was made with $3.50 worth of ordinary surplus parts

After a San Francisco reporter exposed the hoax, Newton and GeBauer were convicted of fraud and sentenced to repay investors. They vanished after a few token payments.

Alien 'crash site' seen in a 2013 satellite image *(Google Earth photo)*

Aztec has profited, though. Until recently the town celebrated UFO Days. In 2011, Scott and Suzanne Ramsey published a book, *The Aztec Incident*, which suggests the Aztec UFO was real and the cover-up continues today.

Today, if you look at satellite images of the crash site, you might see desert rocks arranged in the shape of an alien face, complete with antennae. The rock art—visible from space—was created by local wags.

MURDER ON ROUTE 66
Budville

The Budville Trading Post is on New Mexico 124 (old Route 66), about one mile north of Interstate 40's Exit 104, at GPS 35.06926, -107.525692.

Long before the superslab came through, Howard "Bud" Rice took care of folks. A gritty character in a gritty place, he not only ran one of the few grocery, gas and service stations on this lonely stretch of Route 66, but he was generous with his far-flung neighbors, too. And every Fourth of July, he threw a free barbecue for friends and the state troopers who liked to stop at the Budville Trading Post on their daily patrols.

Just before closing on November 18, 1967, a motorist in a tan compact car pulled up to the Budville pumps. As Bud pumped his gas, the stranger went inside to buy cigarettes from Blanche Brown, the eighty-two-year-old retired schoolteacher who worked Bud's counter.

Bud came inside to find the man arguing with Blanche. But before he could intervene, the man pulled a gun and aimed at Bud. Blanche called for Bud's wife Flossie in the next room and tried in vain to calm the man, who fired five shots. Blanche was hit twice, Bud three times.

As they lay bleeding on the floor, the stranger forced Flossie to give him $450 from the cash register, her purse, and a box of cigars before he turned off the store's lights.

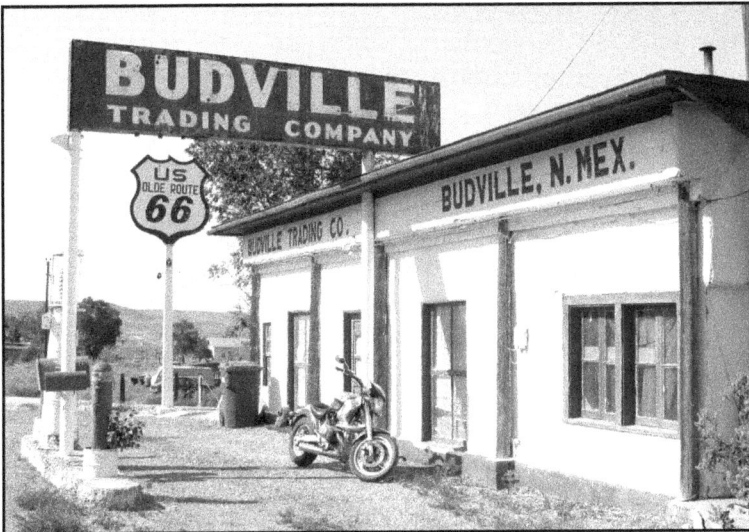

Bud Rice's general store and gas station on old Route 66

In the dark, he tied up Flossie and dragged Bud and Blanche's bodies to the back of the store. He ordered Flossie not to move for fifteen minutes, then sped away.

The Rices' housekeeper, who had hidden during the attack, untied Flossie and called the cops. A frantic manhunt was launched, but the trail quickly went cold.

Eight months later, three felons jailed on unrelated charges were eager to finger the Budville killer. He was Billy Ray White, they said, a twenty-six-year-old drifter, pimp, and career thief. Without a clue to White's whereabouts in the summer of 1968, the FBI put him on its Ten Most Wanted list.

Soon, White was busted in Illinois and brought back to New Mexico for trial. The case against White was purely circumstantial, and most of the prosecution's witnesses were hardened criminals who'd cut sweetheart deals. After only two hours of deliberations, the jury acquitted White.

But White couldn't celebrate. He was immediately extradited to Louisiana to face charges remarkably similar to the Budville murders. He was convicted and sent to Angola State Penitentiary, where he was considered the notorious prison's most feared inmate until he killed himself by slashing his arms with a razor blade in 1974— after reportedly confessing to a fellow inmate that he had, indeed, committed the Budville murders.

Blanche Brown was buried in the Rosebank Cemetery in Calvert, Maryland. Bud Rice was cremated and his ashes were scattered over Route 66 near his trading post.

THE COLDEST CASE
Carlsbad

The crime scene is about twelve miles northwest of Carlsbad, almost a mile off the Queens Highway along a rugged dirt road in a remote desert area at about GPS 32.518925, -104.394244. This is private property.

The summer of '61 was waning. August 11 was one of the last Friday nights before the new school year started, so Carlsbad's teenagers gathered for a last blast.

The Beach was an amusement park on the west bank of the silty Pecos River (GPS 32.42854, -104.220075). For kids, it was the place to be on a Friday night.

Mattie Restine and Patty Sue Pritz, at thirteen and fourteen, were on the verge of womanhood, blossoming between grade school and high school. They were best friends, old enough to go to The Beach without their parents, but still innocent enough to wear matching sailor blouses.

Mattie (left) and Patty Sue

They wandered among the crowd of happy kids, carousel music, and the bright lights of the little midway, waving to friends on the rides and having a good time.

Around 8:40 p.m., they left The Beach and walked toward home. Moments later, a witness saw them visiting with a twentysomething man who'd stopped his light-colored 1955 or '56 Chevy sedan to talk to them. Suddenly, there was a scuffle. One of the girls screamed as the man shoved them into his car and raced away.

State Police, Border Patrol agents, and worried citizens joined local police and deputies in an immediate search, but they couldn't find Mattie and Patty.

Two days later, rabbit hunters stumbled upon the girls' rapidly decomposing bodies in the desert scrub northwest of town. They'd both been shot once in the head with a handgun, possibly a .38, although no shell casings were found at the scene. Police found distinct tire tracks and footprints.

Patty was naked, her Navy-style jumper, pants and underwear fluttering on a nearby mesquite bush. Mattie was still fully clothed. The coroner announced that Mattie had not been raped, and Patty's advanced decomposition prevented him from knowing for certain if she'd been molested. Nevertheless, both families later said the girls had been raped, and the whole town of Carlsbad feared a "sex maniac" was running loose.

Police interviewed a hundred potential suspects, but none panned out. One young Texas man claimed he killed the girls but later proved to be mentally ill. The case went cold.

Over the years, local authorities reassured New Mexicans that Mattie and Patty's murder was still active, but they were no closer to identifying a killer. After the advent of DNA testing—nearly thirty years after the slaying—an investigator briefly boasted that an arrest was

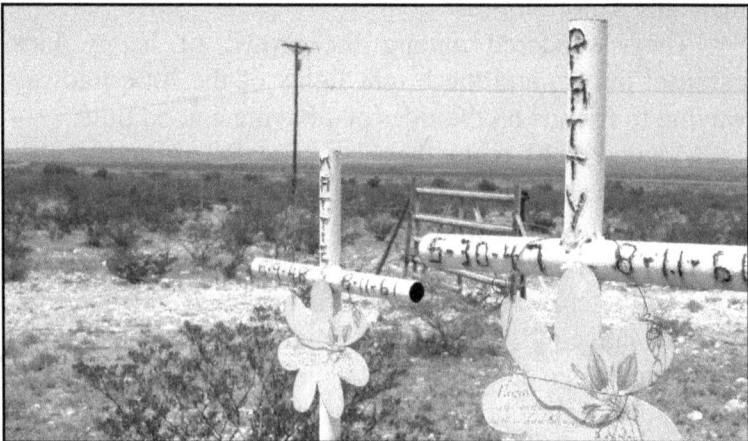

Today, two metal crosses still mark the road near the spot where Mattie and Patty were murdered in 1961.

imminent, but it never happened. Mattie Restine's sister, Anne, is almost singlehandedly keeping the case alive, though she fears the most likely culprits might be dead or dying themselves and will never face justice.

Today, the carnival rides at The Beach are long gone, but their concrete foundations remain visible in the city park's lawns.

Several years ago, two memorial crosses made from steel pipe were erected beside the Queens Highway (GPS 32.509704, -104.389656), marking the turn-off to the spot where the girls' bodies were found. The actual dump site is about seven-tenths of a mile down that road.

Patty Sue Pritz (1947-1961) was buried in the Carlsbad Cemetery, 1506 Boyd Drive. Her grave is in Division I, Block 7, or GPS 32.684238, -105.933967.

Mattie Restine (1948-1961) was originally buried in the Carlsbad Cemetery, then later moved to the Old Bokoshe Memorial Gardens in Bokoshe, Oklahoma.

BONNIE & CLYDE IN NEW MEXICO
Carlsbad
The hideout (torn down in 2006) was at 522 North Sixth Street, or GPS 32.42607, -104.25453.

Depression-era outlaws Bonnie and Clyde roamed a wide range in their short, violent career, but their brief New Mexico vacation-gone-bad is often overlooked by history.

In August 1932, after a fatal shootout with deputies in Oklahoma, the star-crossed lovers needed a safe hideout. They lit out for Carlsbad, where Bonnie Parker's aunt Nellie Stamps lived, reckoning they'd be safe six hundred miles away from the bloody scene of their latest crime.

In Carlsbad, several Parker relatives quietly visited the Stamps house to see the outlaws. But in a secret moment, Nellie tipped off local deputy Joe Johns about her guests.

On August 13, Johns came to investigate, but the tables were quickly turned. Bonnie and Clyde took the deputy hostage and fled, releasing him unharmed in San Antonio the next day. They continued their deadly crime spree for almost two more years, never truly succeeding as bank robbers but capturing a romantic place in crime mythology.

Before sunrise on May 23, 1934, a posse of six Texas and Louisiana lawmen led by Texas Ranger Frank Hamer hid in the bushes on a rural road near Gibsland, Louisiana, where Bonnie and Clyde were expected to pass. When the outlaws stopped their car nearby later that morning, the posse opened fire without warning, killing Bonnie and Clyde instantly.

Bonnie Parker (1910-1934) was buried at Dallas' Crown Hill Memorial Park, 9700 Webb Chapel Road, at GPS 32.86743, -96.86393.

Clyde Barrow (1909-1934) was buried in Dallas' Western Heights Cemetery, 1617 Fort Worth Avenue, at GPS 32.76567, -96.84663.

The Carlsbad house where it all happened was a local landmark for years but fell into disrepair. The town council ordered that the little home and dilapidated outbuildings be torn down in 2006. All that remains today is the crumbling

Iconic outlaw Bonnie Parker's Aunt Nellie nearly got the famous criminal couple arrested in Carlsbad in 1932.

concrete of the front steps.

Nellie Stamps (1882-1944) was buried in Carlsbad Cemetery, 1506 Boyd Drive. Her grave is in Division I, Block 13, Lot 4, or GPS 32.40536, -104.23679.

Joe Johns (1885-1970) went on to become a beloved Eddy County sheriff. He's also buried in the Carlsbad Cemetery, Division K, at GPS 32.40591, -104.23589.

For more about Bonnie and Clyde, see "The Crime Buff's Guide to Outlaw Texas"

A KILLING IN RATTLESNAKE CANYON
Carlsbad area

The Rattlesnake Canyon trailhead is in the Carlsbad Caverns National Park at GPS 32.165591, -104.503302. The dirt road to this site is rugged; a four-wheel-drive vehicle is advised.

David Coughlin and Raffi Kodikian were best friends. In the summer of 1999, these two Bostonians embarked on a cross-country road trip to California, where Coughlin would soon start graduate school.

The two city boys embraced the adventure. On August 4, they pitched camp in Rattlesnake Canyon and planned a hike in the spectacular desert landscape. Packing less than a gallon of water and a map they couldn't read, they were soon lost, dehydrated and delirious.

They foraged for juicy cactus pads, licked rocks and even drank their own urine as they searched for a way out. Kodikian, an aspiring journalist, scribbled a semi-coherent journal of their misadventure.

By the third night, Coughlin began vomiting. Kodikian was frantic. The next day, he wrote in his journal: "I killed & burried [sic] my best friend today. Dave had been in

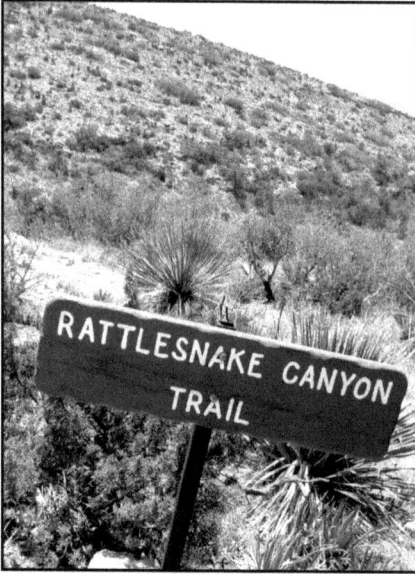

pain all night. At around 5 or 6, he turned to me and begged that I put my knife through his chest. I did, and a second time when he wouldn't die."

Rangers soon found Kodikian, who led them to a pile of rocks where he'd buried Coughlin. Ironically, Coughlin's grave was just 275 feet from the trail, and only a mile and a half from their car. Coughlin's autopsy found him dehydrated but not near death; his vomiting was attributed to eating unripe cactus fruit.

Kodikian, who claimed the two men had reached a death pact on the trail, pleaded guilty to second-degree murder. He served two years in prison. He was released in 2001.

APACHE KID'S GRAVE
Cibola National Forest
This gravesite (GPS 33.6511762, -107.4250363) is nestled in Cyclone Saddle in the rugged Apache Kid Wilderness, which lies within the national forest. The main trail to the Kid's very remote grave marker meanders along thirteen miles of mountain crest. Wear good hiking boots and take plenty of water.

The Apache Kid's real name (*Haskay-bay-nay-ntayl*, or "the tall man destined to come to a mysterious end") is unfamiliar to most, but his enigma lives on. Was he an admired Indian scout or a cold-blooded killer? Was he executed in 1894 by a pursuing posse or did he secretly survive like a ghost and lead borders raids into the 1930s? Was this fugitive genuinely worthy of a 44,000-acre federal wilderness in his name?

Good answers are elusive. Like many of the Wild West's most fascinating figures, fact and myth are inextricably entangled.

He was born an Apache but kidnapped by rival Indians as a boy. When the US cavalry eventually liberated him, the orphan followed Army camps, doing odd jobs and earning the nickname "Kid."

In 1881, he enlisted as a scout when the Army stepped up its efforts against renegade Apache raiders on the border. By 1882, the Kid wore sergeant's stripes … and had developed a fondness for liquor.

At a drunken party in 1887, the Kid murdered a fellow scout and another relative in a revenge killing. During his arrest, a gunfight erupted, and the Kid escaped with several other scouts. They eventually surrendered and were sentenced to life in the military prison at Alcatraz Island (GPS 37.826742, -122.422886).

The scouts' courts-martial were reversed in 1888, but they were soon re-arrested by outraged civilian authorities and sentenced to the Yuma Territorial Prison (GPS 32.727342, -114.615068) for seven years.

They never arrived. Along the way, the Kid and his fellow convicts killed Sheriff Glen Reynolds and escaped again. (Sheriff Reynolds was buried in the Globe Cemetery, GPS 33.39477, -110.79434).

It would be the last time anyone officially saw the Apache Kid.

Over the next few years, many people claimed to have seen the Kid leading Apache raids on ranchers and freighters, or kidnapping white women for his pleasure. More crimes than he could have possibly committed were attributed to him. A $5,000 bounty—more than $25,000 in today's dollars—was placed on his head.

In 1894, a posse of angry ranchers reportedly killed the Apache Kid at a remote spot called Cyclone Saddle in the San Mateo Mountains. They shot him and left his body unburied to be eaten by wolves. They blazed a tree to mark the spot, and that scar can still be seen today.

But legends don't die so easy. Many have argued the Kid wasn't killed at Cyclone Saddle but lived well into the Twentieth century among his Apache faithful in the Sierra Madre Occidental.

ST. JAMES HOTEL
Cimarron
The St. James Hotel is at 617 South Collison Avenue, or GPS 36.505, -104.920556.

First, a little language lesson is in order: "Cimarron" is Spanish for "wild" and "untamed." And that's exactly what boomtown Cimarron was in the 1870s when Henry Lambert arrived.

Lambert had been President Lincoln's personal chef, but after Lincoln's assassination, he drifted West to seek his fortune in the Cimarron gold fields. He proved to be a bad prospector but a consummate hotelier.

In 1872, Lambert opened the doors of a tavern that would soon become his St. James Hotel, providing room and board for Santa Fe Trail travelers, vagabonds, adventurers … and outlaws.

The St. James Hotel was as untamed as Cimarron itself. Twenty-six men were killed there—eleven by notorious shootist Clay Allison alone (and two by Lambert himself). Townsfolk commonly asked every morning, "Who was killed at Lambert's last night?"

The hotel's guestbook reads like a history of the Wild West (and might be just as mythic). Listed among the lodgers are Buffalo Bill, Jesse James (and his assassin Bob Ford), Wyatt Earp, Frederic Remington, Bat Masterson, *Ben-Hur* author Lew Wallace, Sheriff Pat Garrett and Billy the Kid (not together), Doc Holliday, Kit Carson, Annie Oakley, General Phil Sheridan, writer Zane Grey, and train robber "Black Jack" Ketchum.

Some of those definitely spent at least one night in the St. James. Others might be figments of imaginative marketing, but Wild West history is half legend anyway.

One legend is that Clay Allison led a mob in lynching suspected serial killer Charles Kennedy in neighboring Elizabethtown and later brought Kennedy's severed head to Lambert, who displayed it in his saloon. When the head got a little too ripe, it was moved to a fence post outside, where it sat until it disappeared.

The hotel claims one permanent resident: the ghost of murder victim T.J. Wright, who reportedly won the St. James in a poker game but was shot in the back by an

Faces of famous Old West figures, like Wyatt Earp (l) line the hallways of the historic St. James Hotel in Cimarron.

unknown killer when he returned to his room (No. 18). It's not clear what this saddle-tramp was wagering that Lambert would risk his beloved hotel, but nevermind.

And if the haunting isn't creepy enough, an original headstone in the lobby commemorates the 1875 slaying of beloved Parson Franklin Tolby, who was killed in the bitter Colfax County range war. Tolby is also buried in the Clayton cemetery, beneath a bigger, newer marker.

Stepping into the St. James is a trip backward in time. It is decorated in classic Victorian style with antique

Henry Lambert's grave in the Cimarron Cemetery

chandeliers, thick velvet drapes, brocade wallpaper, and many of the hotel's original furnishings. Its dining room—the original saloon—still has Lambert's first bar ... and twenty-two purported bullet holes in its pressed-tin ceiling.

(The story goes that Lambert installed extra-thick wooden ceilings in his saloon to protect guests in rooms above from being shot by drunken *pistoleros* below.)

Henry Lambert (1838-1913) is buried in the Cimarron Cemetery at GPS 36.50021, -104.92818.

These days, Cimarron has settled down, but the historic St. James is still the liveliest place in town. The hotel occasionally hosts "murder mystery weekends" where guests play some of the famous people who lodged there (or not).

See "Charles Kennedy, Serial Killer" (Elizabethtown)

DAVY CROCKETT, OUTLAW
Cimarron
The Cimarron Cemetery is on a hill about one mile southwest of town, just west of New Mexico 21. Crockett's purported grave is at GPS 36.50028, -104.92779.

Davy Crockett (1853-1876) was the bully of Cimarron. His namesake uncle had been a hero of the Alamo, but young Davy was bad to the bone.

Outlaw Davy Crockett's purported Cimarron grave

A prison escapee from Texas, Crockett came west to Cimarron. He fell in with the equally wicked gunslinger Clay Allison, with whom he shared a special hatred of blacks, especially Buffalo Soldiers stationed nearby.

In one incident, a drunken Crockett gunned down three Buffalo Soldiers in Henry Lambert's saloon. The judge forgave the fatal shooting because of Crockett's drunkenness, and instead fined him $50 for carrying a gun against town law.

It didn't slow Crockett down. He reportedly grew more belligerent, sometimes extorting drinks at gunpoint and riding his horse into saloons. More than one of the bullet holes that still exist in the St. James Hotel saloon's pressed-tin ceiling came from Crockett's guns.

On September 30, 1876, twenty-three-year-old Crockett was shot while resisting arrest. He was buried in an unmarked grave in the Cimarron Cemetery. Today, a headstone has been erected, but it's unknown if it marks the actual spot where the young outlaw was buried.

'BLACK JACK' LOSES HIS HEAD
Clayton

The Clayton Cemetery is east of town on Princeton Avenue. The grave is at GPS 36.44557, -103.16404.

Thomas "Black Jack" Ketchum (1863-1901) and his brother Sam lived and died on the outlaw trail. They rode with the Wild Bunch, robbed trains and shopkeepers, and killed innocent people.

Black Jack is suspected in the 1896 disappearance of Albert Jennings Fountain and his son. He also murdered storekeeper Levi Herzstein after an 1896 burglary in Liberty. (Herzstein is buried in the Montefiore Cemetery in Las Vegas, New Mexico; his grave is in Row 4, Block F, at GPS 35.59548, -105.23962).

Black Jack Ketchum's 'new' grave is a Clayton tourist attraction.

Sam was mortally wounded in an 1899 train robbery near Folsom, New Mexico, and died a few days later in Santa Fe's territorial prison.

In 1899, just a few weeks after Sam's death, Black Jack

staged another robbery of the same train. But he was wounded in a shootout with the shotgun-wielding conductor and captured. After his tattered arm was amputated, Black Jack was convicted and sentenced to die.

Black Jack's 1901 hanging was a big event. Tickets were sold, and hawkers peddled little Black Jack dolls hanging on a souvenir stick. Crowds gathered around the hangman's scaffold in the yard behind the old Union County jail (a plaque marks the spot where the scaffold stood at the Sheriff's Office, Adams and South Second streets, GPS 36.449117, -103.187719) to watch the one-armed outlaw hang. Among them was Morris Herzstein, whose brother Levi had been killed by the Ketchums. And a photographer stood ready to snap the dangling body.

As he perched on the trap door, the infamous robber spoke his last words. "Good-bye," he said. "Please dig my grave very deep. All right, hurry up."

The trap door sprung and Black Jack plunged through. But as he hit the end of the rope, his neck snapped and his head flew off. The photographer got his picture, now a ghastly artifact of the Wild West: Black Jack's headless corpse sprawled on the ground with his hooded head lying nearby.

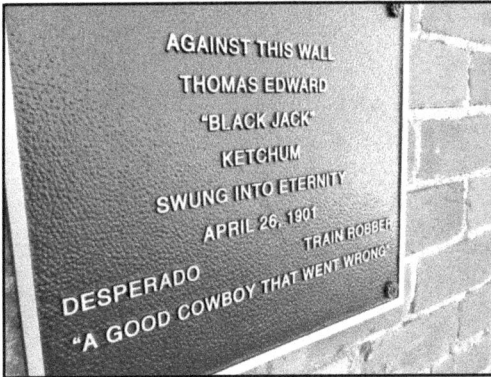

A historical plaque marks the exact spot of Black Jack's grisly hanging just outside the Union County sheriff's office, still in use today.

A local doctor stitched Black Jack's head back on his neck and he was buried unceremoniously in a pasture. But in the 1930s, when a state road project planned to run right over the unmarked grave, Black Jack was dug up.

A handful of citizens opened the old casket and found the outlaw's body had been well-preserved. A cowboy pal put flowers in the coffin with a note: "To a cowboy who went wrong."

Black Jack was reburied on the edge of the Clayton Cemetery without a marker, away from proper folks. But the cemetery grew and like many western towns, Clayton eventually recognized the outlaw's tourism value. His now-elaborately marked grave sits smack-dab in the center of the cemetery, where it is the most visited tourist attraction in this entire town.

See also "Outlaw Sam Ketchum's Grave" (Santa Fe)

THE COLUMBUS RAID
Columbus
Columbus is 35 miles south of Deming on New Mexico 11. The US Customs House museum and visitor center is across New Mexico Highway 11 from the depot, at GPS 31.827990, -107.640644.

In the days after 9/11, the news reported breathlessly that these were the first terror attacks on American soil. It wasn't true.

In the wee hours of March 9, 1916, a small army of Mexican insurgents led by rebel General Francisco "Pancho" Villa raided the sleepy border town of Columbus, New Mexico.

The fiercest fighting was concentrated in the streets around the Hoover Hotel (GPS 31.830389, -107.637272) and the two-story, brick Columbus school (GPS 31.836203,

-107.638796), where many women and children took shelter from the raging battle. Other citizens fired at the Villistas from their homes and shops.

The raiders looted and burned many houses. For most of the ninety-minute battle, Villa watched from a nearby hill (GPS 31.826503, -107.641702), surrounded by snipers who were firing into the town.

After a handful of 13th Cavalry soldiers from nearby Camp Furlong (GPS 31.827523, -107.640758) set up machine guns in the center of town, Villa's men suffered heavy casualties and retreated back across the border.

In the end, seventy-three Villistas and eighteen American soldiers and civilians were killed. Three of the American victims were buried in the Valley Heights Cemetery west of town (GPS 31.83658, -107.66250); the others were shipped to national cemeteries or hometown churchyards. The raiders' corpses were piled together with

Columbus' Hoover Hotel, site of some of the fiercest action during the 1916 raid by Pancho Villa, still stands today in the peaceful little village.

their dead horses east of town, soaked with gasoline, and burned.

The Columbus Raid sparked General John "Jack" Pershing's so-called Pancho Villa Expedition into Mexico only days later. This punitive expedition dispatched 11,000 troops and became a testing ground for new technology—including air surveillance and motorized tactics that would be used by American troops in World War I. After almost a year of searching, seventeen soldiers died but failed to find Villa.

In one of many eerie parallels to the hunt for Osama bin Laden eighty-five years later, Villa hid from US soldiers in remote caves and at one point watched as an American unit passed.

Pancho Villa mounted the first terrorist raid on American soil

Villa retired peaceably from his revolutionary life in 1920 but was assassinated by a rival Mexican gang while riding in his car on July 20, 1923. He was originally buried in his hometown of Parral, but his body might have been moved later to Mexico City.

In 1926, a grave-robber decapitated Villa's corpse and stole his head. One unconfirmed story is that it now sits among other famous people's skulls in the catacombs of Yale's secret Skull and Bones Society.

Today, Columbus' star tourist attraction is the Pancho Villa State Park, named for the town's nemesis. Several historic buildings from the time of the raid still stand in Columbus, including the US Customs House museum, the Hoover Hotel, the school, two adobe structures and the Camp Furlong Recreation Hall.

SERIAL KILLER ON THE TRAIL
Elizabethtown

Charles Kennedy's grave is somewhere the Elizabethtown Cemetery, off Colfax County Road B-20. A weathered but more recent marker is in the cemetery's northeast corner, at GPS 36.62088, -105.28551.

Charles Kennedy (1839-1870) ran an Old West version of the Bates Motel. Travelers on the road between the town of Elizabethtown and Taos commonly stopped at his isolated roadhouse for a bed and a meal. Unfortunately, some checked in and never checked out.

Kennedy would murder his guests, steal their money and possessions, then bury or burn their corpses. At a time when countless numbers of strangers were streaming into the territory, they were never missed.

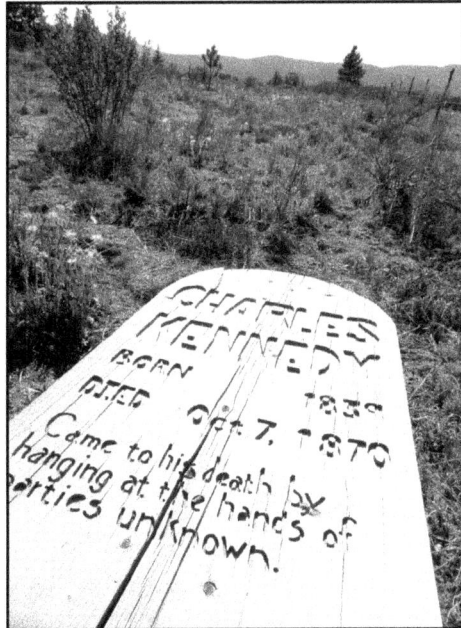

Then in 1870, a bloodied woman stumbled into the Elizabethtown saloon where notorious gunfighter Clay Allison, highwayman Davey Crockett (a nephew of the Alamo hero) and others were drinking. She told

Charles Kennedy's reputed grave marker at Elizabethtown

how her husband waylaid his victims—possibly as many as fourteen.

When Allison and the others investigated, they found ample proof of her claims. They collected charred bones from the fireplace and two skeletons from the cellar. Later, another skull turned up.

Kennedy was arrested, but before he could stand trial, Allison and Crockett led a mob of vigilantes who snatched Kennedy from the jail and lynched him. Legend says Allison decapitated Kennedy and gifted his head to Henry Lambert at the St. James Hotel in Cimarron (617 South Collison Avenue, or GPS 36.505, -104.920556). The putrefying skull was reportedly displayed in the St. James' saloon until it got intolerably rotten, then moved to a fence post outside, where it sat until it disappeared forever.

The rest of the serial killer's body was buried outside the cemetery fence when Elizabethtown's citizens refused to bury him among proper folks.

See also "St. James Hotel" (Cimarron)

THE BONE THIEF
Fort Craig
The historic Fort Craig Cemetery is about 100 miles south of Albuquerque, just east of Interstate 25, at GPS 33.630859, -107.01145. This is a remote site on federal property.

Dee Brecheisen (1938-2004) was a decorated Vietnam veteran, a retired Air Force lieutenant colonel, an airline pilot, and a respected amateur historian.

He was also a prolific grave-robber.

In 2004, a tipster told federal authorities that Brecheisen had been digging up graves in the abandoned

Fort Craig cemetery for artifacts and human remains. In fact, the informant said, he'd once seen a mummified Buffalo Soldier in a military uniform stored in Brecheisen's home.

Fort Craig was established before the Civil War. In 1862, Union troopers fought the Battle of Valverde just two miles north, and some 100 Yankee war dead were buried in the fort cemetery. Later, during the Indian Wars, regiments of the famed Buffalo Soldiers—black cavalry troops—were based there.

All the dead soldiers in the Fort Craig cemetery were supposedly exhumed and moved to national cemeteries elsewhere in the late 1800s, but records were so bad, it was nearly impossible to know if all the graves had been found.

They hadn't. Ground-penetrating radar later revealed the Army had overlooked up to 100 coffins that still

This unassuming suburban house stored the illicit, sometimes grisly, collection of Indian and Old West military artifacts looted by a former war hero.

contained human bodies.

By the time federal agents got moving, Brecheisen was dead of Lou Gehrig's Disease. A raid at his home (10 Park Lane in Peralta, at GPS 34.832633, -106.704886) uncovered a grim treasure trove of grave loot, from military buttons and Civil War-era gun parts to assorted bones and buckets of Indian potshards. Piles of plunder filled Brecheisen's garden beds.

The centerpiece of it all was the mummified skull of a Buffalo Soldier, which still had skin and a mat of hair. It was later identified as the head of Private Thomas Smith, a former slave who'd died of cholera at Fort Craig in 1866.

Smith's remains were reburied in Santa Fe National Cemetery

Brecheisen's looting went far beyond Fort Craig. Investigators say he also dug up graves in Fort Thorn and Fort Conrad in southern New Mexico, plus ancient Native American burial sites in the Four Corners area. They suspect he also stole a Fort Craig burial map from the National Archives and spotted his targets from the air.

To thwart further pillaging, federal archaeologists exhumed more than 60 Fort Craig graves in 2007 and buried them elsewhere with proper markers.

The wayward skull of Private Thomas Smith (1843-1866) was reburied with full military honors at the Santa Fe National Cemetery in 2009. His grave is in Section 15A, Site 25. He and two identified comrades were buried beside many unidentified remains from Fort Craig's cemetery, memorialized with a half-ton granite-and-bronze marker at GPS 35.700967, -105.94627.

Other exhumed soldiers were buried at the Fort Leavenworth National Cemetery.

Brecheisen was buried with military honors in the Clearfield Cemetery in Eudora, Kansas.

BACK FROM THE DEAD
Hachita
Hachita Cemetery is a little more than one mile south of Hachita on New Mexico 81, GPS 31.899825, -108.319133.

William Walters (d. 1921) was a better cowboy than outlaw, and that's why they called him "Bronco Bill."

But ranching didn't thrill him, so Bronco Bill embarked on a desperado's existence. For a long time, he was a miserable failure at it, going to jail more often than making a big score. It got so bad that he actually went back to being a cowboy for a while before drifting back to a life of small-time crime. He briefly rode with Tom "Black Jack" Ketchum and supposedly killed a couple men, but he quit to start his own gang.

Between 1894 and 1897, Walters hit a career high point. His loosely knit gang scored hits on several small Wells Fargo shipments.

Then in 1898, he and another crook named "Kid" Johnson robbed a Belen mail train of $50,000 in heavy bags of coins. Weighted down by their loot, they only escaped by burying the money somewhere west of town and killing most of their pursuers. But a new posse soon caught up with the two outlaws and another gunfight erupted. Both were shot dead and their corpses hauled back to camp.

But when the sheriff yanked Bronco Bill's dead legs, the outlaw gasped and suddenly started breathing again.

41

The startled lawman sent a message to the nearest town: "Send a doctor and a coffin."

Bronco Bill was jailed in the territorial prison for life, but he was pardoned after he told a reporter he was quitting crime for good. The killer went back to being a cowboy and curiously never returned to Belen for any of his alleged loot. He died as an old man when he fell out of a windmill and broke his neck.

Walters was originally buried without a headstone in Hachita, although a simple marker exists today that might (or might not) mark his actual grave.

TEEN KILLS HIS FAMILY
Hondo

The Chavez Canyon Ranch crime scene is on Lincoln County Road E023 two miles northeast of Hondo, at GPS 33.39320, -105.24833. This is a remote private property.

Paul Posey was the foreman on the Chavez Canyon Ranch owned by ABC newsman Sam Donaldson. He lived there with his fourteen-year-old son Cody, his third wife Tryone, and thirteen-year-old stepdaughter Marilea Schmid.

A longtime rancher, Paul ran the place with an iron fist. Everybody had chores, and Paul could be tough if they weren't done right. And young teenager Cody bore the brunt of it.

But there might have been deeper, darker secrets on the isolated ranch.

On July 4, 2004, Paul exploded because Cody wasn't cleaning the horse stalls fast enough. He slapped his son across the face.

When Paul left the barn, Cody took a .38-caliber pistol from his step-sister's saddlebag, removed its snake-shot cartridges, and loaded it with deadlier bullets. He then went into the house, where his stepmother Tryone was in the living room reading a book. He shot her twice in the head.

When Paul and Marilea heard the shots, they ran to the house. Cody shot them both in the head, too.

He dragged the corpses to the yard, where he loaded them in the bucket of a John Deere backhoe. He first tried to dig a hole in an open patch of ground, but couldn't break the ground. So he buried their bodies in the ranch's manure pile.

Cody changed his clothes, drove into town to buy a soda pop, tossed the murder weapon in the river, and went to a friend's house.

The bloody scene was discovered by Donaldson himself when he couldn't reach Paul Posey by phone. Three days after the killing, Cody was arrested.

Stepsister Marilea Schmid (1991-2004) was buried at the small Tinnie Cemetery (GPS 33.371309, -105.221850). Paul and Tryone Posey were cremated and their ashes given to family.

At his 2006 trial, Cody said he had simply grown tired of his father's physical

Marilea Schmidt's grave in Tinnie

and mental abuse. Cody claimed that the night before the slayings, his father had summoned him to the master bedroom and tried to force him to have sex with his stepmother. When he refused, Cody claimed he was burned with a welding rod. A string of friends and ranch hands also testified that Paul Posey was an abusive father.

The prosecution argued Cody was a lying sociopath who invented wild stories about abuse. If Cody was merely defending himself from his antagonists, why did he kill his younger stepsister?

A jury convicted Cody of first-degree murder for killing his stepsister, Marilea; second-degree murder for his stepmother; and manslaughter for his father. Prosecutors asked that Cody go to prison for life, without the possibility of parole, but the judge sentenced Cody—then sixteen—as a juvenile. He could be locked up only until he was 21.

In June 2010, relatives of Posey's victims won an $87 million wrongful death civil lawsuit against him, seeking mainly to limit his ability to make any money from selling his story.

A few months later, on his twenty-first birthday, Cody Posey walked out of juvenile hall a free man.

A TERRORIST'S BIRTHPLACE
Las Cruces
Anwar al-Awlaki's childhood home is at 313 Fite Street, at GPS 32.276880, -106.750214.

On April 22, 1971, a bouncing baby boy was born to Mr. and Mrs. Nasser al-Awlaki. Dad was a Fulbright Scholar studying for a master's degree in agricultural economics at New Mexico State University, and the couple named their new son Anwar.

The next year, the al-Awlakis moved to Nebraska, where Nasser earned a doctorate and then got a job as a professor at a Minnesota university. The whole family moved back home to Yemen in 1978, when little Anwar was just seven.

In 1991, Anwar came back to the US to get an engineering degree at Colorado State University—and spent his summers training with Islamist insurgents in Afghanistan. After graduating from college, he studied at San Diego State University and George Washington University. While in San Diego, he preached at a mosque, where he met two future 9/11 hijackers.

In 2001, Anwar became an imam at a Virginia mosque, where he met Major Nidal Hasan, who would kill thirteen and wound twenty-nine in the 2009 Fort Hood mass murder. As he became more openly radicalized, he also drew attention from authorities.

In 2002, Anwar moved to the UK, and then in 2004, back to Yemen, where he led the al Qaeda unit that

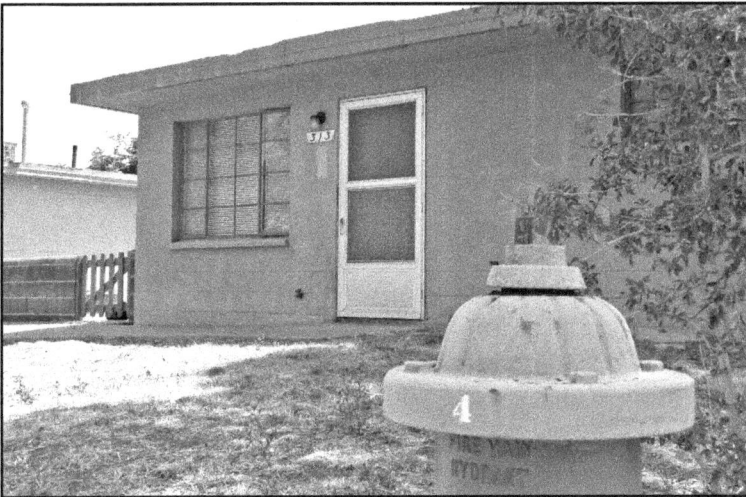

Al Qaeda terrorist Anwar al-Awlaki's father was a grad student at NMSU in Las Cruces when Anwar was born in 1971. They lived at this little house on campus.

executed the abortive 2009 underwear bombing of a US airliner and called for the death of a Norwegian cartoonist who dared to draw the Prophet Muhammad, among other terrorist attacks.

Al-Awlaki was now one of America's most wanted terrorists and, as an American cleric, one of al Qaeda's most effective propagandists. After considerable debate over the legality of assassinating US citizens, President Barack Obama approved orders to kill him.

On Sept. 30, 2011, two CIA Predator drones fired Hellfire missiles into a car in Yemen, incinerating al-Awlaki; American Samir Khan, who edited an English-language Al Qaeda web magazine called "Inspire"; and two others.

A year later, al-Awlaki's sixteen-year-old Denver-born son was killed in another drone strike in Yemen.

CRICKET COOGLER, COLD CASE
Las Cruces

Masonic Cemetery is at 760 South Compress Road. The grave is in Section 5, Block 13, GPS 32.30076, -106.78536.

Ovida Coogler—"Cricket" to her friends—loved to party. She was an eighteen-year-old waitress who'd been hanging around bars since she was fourteen. She was mired in the hard life of a farmtown barfly, but set her sights on much more, so she liked to frolic with powerful men who enjoyed Las Cruces' illegal but openly thriving gambling houses. She flitted along the dark edge of widespread corruption, looking for a way out of her dismal life.

Unfortunately, she found it.

A couple weeks after she disappeared on March 31, 1949, her rotting corpse was found in a shallow desert grave south of town (in the area of 32.188725, -106.685815). She'd apparently been raped and run down by a car, but Sheriff "Happy" Apodaca mysteriously refused to authorize an autopsy. On her death certificate, under "cause of death," there appears only a question mark.

Then Apodaca arrested a startling suspect: Pittsburgh Steelers' rookie halfback Jerry Nuzum, a New Mexico football legend. He'd been seen with Coogler outside the rough Del Rio Bar (formerly at GPS 32.30914, -106.77844) on the night she went missing.

The ruthless Apodaca cajoled, threatened, and deceived Nuzum, who steadfastly maintained his innocence. He was released only after students at New Mexico State University raised enough signatures to

Visitors still leave flowers at Cricket Coogler's grave in Las Cruces, more than 60 years after she was murdered.

convene a grand jury, which cleared Nuzum.

And Apodaca also arrested a black man, Wesley Byrd, and held him in jail for ten days without telling anyone. Seeking a confession, the sheriff tortured Byrd by squeezing his testicles with a bike lock.

Despite those atrocities, Byrd wasn't indicted for Cricket Coogler's killing.

But in 1950, Governor Edwin Mechem, who had campaigned for office on the Coogler case and also loved the corrupt playground in Las Cruces, pressured Apodaca to pin it all on the football hero Nuzum. The Steelers' running back was charged and his trial was covered nationwide.

Nuzum admitted he'd tried to give Coogler a ride and she resisted; a local trucker stopped Nuzum from manhandling her. But two local cops testified seeing Coogler get into a two-tone Chevrolet—possibly bearing official state license plates—at Church and Bowman streets (GPS 32.308249, -106.777202) two hours later. And when Coogler's body was exhumed from her Masonic Cemetery grave to be re-examined, the coroner found she'd been covered in quicklime, destroying any evidence that her remains might have yielded.

Finally, Nuzum's defense found a bombshell witness who claimed to see two State Police officers chase and beat Coogler before throwing her in their car.

The judge quickly threw out the case against Jerry Nuzum.

Around the same time, a federal jury convicted Sheriff Apodaca and New Mexico State Police Chief Hubert Beasley of violating Wesley Byrd's civil rights when they tortured him. Each served a year in prison, but both were pardoned by President Harry Truman.

In the end, Coogler's unsolved murder revealed serious corruption in New Mexico's political and law enforcement establishments, although both good and bad people were damaged in the process.

Nuzum played only four seasons of football and died of cancer in Pittsburgh in 1997. He was seventy-three. Late in life, he told a reporter he'd been forever stained by the false accusation.

Locals have long believed Sheriff "Happy" Apodaca (1912-1981) killed Coogler or knew who did, and tried valiantly to cover it up. He died of a heart attack at age sixty-nine, and is also buried in Las Cruces' Masonic Cemetery in Section 6, Block 15, or GPS 32.30078, -106.78566.

Edwin Mechem (1912-2002) served eight years as governor and two years as a US senator and federal judge. He's buried in Albuquerque's Fairview Memorial Park at GPS 35.07023, -106.61930, where his simple marker doesn't mention his storied political career.

Author Paula Moore covers the case in her 2008 book *Cricket in the Web*.

BOWLING ALLEY MASSACRE
Las Cruces
The crime scene is at the former Las Cruces Bowl, 1201 East Amador Avenue, or GPS 32.309978, -106.766948.

On the bright Saturday morning of February 10, 1990, two men strolled into Las Cruces Bowl an hour before it opened. The manager was there doing some paperwork with her 12-year-old daughter. A 13-year-old employee, Amy Houser, did busywork at the desk. The alley's cook was preparing for a busy day, assumed the two Hispanic guys were part of a cleaning crew.

But they weren't.

One of the men brandished a pistol and herded everyone into a back office. They screamed at their hostages to keep their heads down while the robbers—one in his late 20s and the other a middle-aged man—ransacked the place, frantically searching cabinets and looking for cash.

Agitated by the unexpected number of people they found there, the robbers finally discovered up to $5,000 in an unlocked safe—just as lane-mechanic Steven Teran unwittingly walked into a massacre with his two-year-old daughter and 6-year-old stepdaughter.

The robbers shot everyone at point-blank range, execution-style. After 25 shots, four people lay dead: Teran, his two little girls, and 13-year-old Amy Houser. Everyone else was seriously wounded. One of the survivors, the manager's 12-year-old daughter, was shot three times but managed to call 911. But by the time police arrived, the killers were long gone.

The mass killing that happened at this bowling alley in 1990 remains unsolved more than 20 years later.

The mass murder has never been solved.

Amy Houser (1976-1990) was buried in Section 9, Block 16 of Las Cruces' Masonic Cemetery, at GPS 32.30130, -106.78626.

Steve Teran (1963-1990) was buried with his girls, Valerie and Paula, in Section A, Block 113 of Silver City's Memory Lane Cemetery, at GPS 32.78337, -108.25573.

LOS LUNAS DECALOGUE STONE
Los Lunas
This boulder is in a remote area about fifteen miles due west of Los Lunas along New Mexico 6 at GPS 34.785217, -106.996512. To hike to this spot on state land, you must buy a $25 recreational access permit from the New Mexico State Land Office. They'll give you a map.

Outlawry is about breaking rules. And the original rules—the Ten Commandments—were carved in stone. In the Holy Land. More than seven thousand miles away from the village of Los Lunas, New Mexico.

So imagine the shock of finding the Ten Commandments carved into the flat face of a 100-ton basalt boulder on the side of Hidden Mountain, near Los Lunas. More startling yet, they're carved in Hebrew (mixed with a little Greek).

The rock was discovered in 1933 by Dr. Frank Hibben, a University of New Mexico archaeologist who was led to the site by an old man who claimed to have stumbled upon it in the 1880s.

Did members of a lost tribe of Israel find their way to the desert that would become known as New Mexico? Some people think so. The inscription has been estimated to be between 500 and 2,000 years old.

Others dismiss it as a hoax, full of the kind of Paleo-Hebrew punctuation and spelling errors that frustrate all of us. And archaeologists point out that no other North American evidence of ancient Hebrew culture—settlements, tools, writing, bones or artwork—has ever been found.

Fake or fact? Nobody knows.

PEACE, LOVE, MURDER
Placitas

The former site of the Lower Farms Commune is at GPS 35.302752, -106.406933. This is private property.

In the 1960s and '70s, Placitas was a far-out satellite in the hippie universe, man. Literally.

At the groovy height of the Love Generation, hundreds of long-haired, seldom-washed, sandal-footed kids flocked to communes in this northern New Mexico village to escape society's rules, smoke a little bud, grow their own food, and seek the meaning of life. They lived in yurts, adobe shacks, geodesic domes, and dozens of communes with names like Sun Farm, Freeform, and Long John's Valley nestled in the piñon hills. Everything was copasetic.

Ulysses S. Grant was the main man at the Lower Farms commune east of town. The friendly, slightly insane Grant claimed to be the reincarnation of the famous Civil War general and 18th president (a fact that he believed entitled him to free stamps at the Placitas post office and a federal pension). Grant also ran for New Mexico governor in 1969, appearing for cameras in Civil War-style pants and riding a white horse named Blue.

But the mellow got harshed in 1970. As more drugs and less idealistic people moved in, the Placitas utopia grew funky. Two badass hippies, Robert Copeland and

George Jonas, reportedly wanted to take over Grant's Lower Farms commune, and Grant fought back.

On December 1, Grant lured the two men to a hidden spot in the hills and shot them dead. The next morning, Grant and his wife vanished.

The FBI was flummoxed. The murderous hippie had disappeared into thin air.

Eighteen years later, the mystery broke. In the rubble of a house fire near Bonner's Ferry, Idaho, deputies found two bodies. Both had been shot and the fire intentionally set. They were identified as Donald Waskey and his wife Helen, aka Mr. and Mrs. Ulysses S. Grant.

In a nearby barn (about five miles east of Bonner's Ferry at GPS 48.675241, -116.22286), investigators found more than a thousand thriving marijuana plants—the biggest indoor pot farm Idaho had ever seen—along with a cache of assault weapons, machine guns and rifles with night-vision scopes. They also found booby traps throughout the facility, later estimated to have produced almost $2 million worth of pot every month.

Nobody has ever been arrested for the murders.

Bummer.

The former Lower Farms commune is now a private home.

Elfego Baca's grave in Albuquerque's Sunset Memorial

THE FRISCO SHOOTOUT
Reserve
The historic Frisco Store still exists in Lower San Francisco Plaza along New Mexico 435, at GPS 33.692601, -108.767416.

At different times in his colorful life, Elfego Baca (1865-1945) was a gunfighter, lawman, politician, and lawyer. He was also involved in one of the Old West's most awesome shootouts.

In 1884, Baca—still a teenager—ordered a fake sheriff's badge, stole some guns, and named himself sheriff of Socorro County, New Mexico. His main job was corralling the drunken cowboys who'd get a little too wild on Saturday nights.

In October of his first year as sheriff, Baca arrested a drunk cowboy. But when the barkeep refused to press charges, the incensed Baca took the cowboy hostage.

Cowboys and lawmen converged on Lower San Francisco Plaza. During the negotiations for the cowboy's freedom, Baca shot one of his hostage's friends. A local judge got involved, and just when the whole bloody affair seemed to be settled, Baca fled into a nearby house (now the historic Frisco Store) with the cowboy's guns.

As many as 80 cowboys surrounded the adobe shack where Baca hid. Legend says they fired more than four thousand shots into the structure, but Baca was unscathed.

The siege lasted 33 hours. Four cowboys were killed and eight wounded by the time Baca surrendered.

Baca was tried for the first killing and acquitted. A piece of evidence in his trial was the front door of his hideout, which had four hundred bullet holes.

He went on to be a real sheriff, US marshal, prosecutor, and defense attorney. He was fond of saying he defended 30 alleged killers and only one went to prison.

Baca died in 1945 and is buried in Albuquerque's Sunset Memorial Park, 924 Menaul Boulevard NE. His grave is in the arid Santa Barbara section at GPS 35.10878, -106.63444.

In 1958, Disney produced a TV miniseries called *The Nine Lives of Elfego Baca*, starring Robert Loggia.

THE OUTLAW POLITICIAN
Near Ruidoso
Albert Fall's former Three Rivers Ranch is fifteen miles west of Ruidoso, at GPS 33.38694, -105.93111. This is a remote site and private property.

Not all New Mexico outlaws used guns. Some, like Albert Fall (1861-1944), used their wits.

At a glance, his career in New Mexico appears sterling. He was a US Senator and New Mexico Supreme Court justice who became Secretary of the Interior under President Warren G. Harding in 1921-1923. But his moral ambiguities were signs of bigger trouble to come.

It wasn't that this lawyer had successfully defended rank criminals such as the accused killers of his nemesis Albert Jennings Fountain and his son, or the suspected killer of legendary lawman Pat Garrett. Instead, it was a willingness to cut political and legal corners to benefit himself.

Political bad guy Albert B. Fall

In 1929, the chickens came home to roost when Fall was convicted of accepting bribes of $385,000 to grant his oil friends access to naval reserves at Teapot Dome, Wyoming. The scandal was just one more blow to the public trust, rocked just a few years before by baseball's Black Sox scandal — and gave us a new slang term: "fall guy." Fall was convicted, fined $100,000 and imprisoned for a year — the first American Cabinet secretary ever to go to prison for misconduct in office.

His beloved Three Rivers Ranch was seized by creditors, along with most of his assets. Disgraced and impoverished, he died in his sleep four days after his eighty-third birthday. He is buried in El Paso's Evergreen Alameda Cemetery, 4371 Alameda Avenue. His grave is in Section K, Lot 211 (GPS 31.77337, -106.44018).

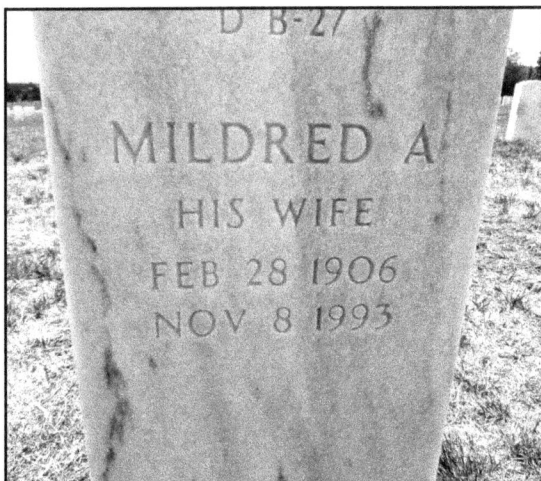

Millie Cusey was buried with her late husband at the Fort Bayard National Cemetery

THOROUGHLY MADAM MILLIE
Silver City

The Fort Bayard National Cemetery is at 200 Camino De Paz, in Fort Bayard, about seven miles east of Silver City. Millie Cusey's grave is in Section D, Row B, Site 27, or GPS 32.79976, -108.15446.

Mildred Clark Cusey (1906-1993) was orphaned at a young age and shuttled with her sister through a series of Kansas City foster homes. When her sister was diagnosed with tuberculosis, Millie scooped her up and moved to New Mexico, where she supported both of them by working as a "Harvey Girl," the nickname of waitresses at the Harvey House railroad restaurants.

But as her sister's medical bills grew, the teenage Millie needed faster cash. Servicing randy travelers in back rooms proved just the trick (pun intended).

Ambitious young Millie started dreaming of running her own bordello—sooner rather than later. By her late twenties, she owned six brothels, including three in Silver

City alone (now gone at 500-514 Hudson Street, or GPS 32.771606, -108.27494).

In fact, by the time she died, this tireless entrepreneur had owned a ranch, restaurants, beauty parlors, bars and parking lots throughout the state.

Millie had a reputation as a fair and honest madam who protected her girls fiercely. She didn't allow drugs or booze, and she supported local charities generously.

After Millie retired in 1978, she hosted a huge rummage sale to unload thousands of artifacts from her profitable life of ill repute. She retired to Santa Clara, where she had also run a thriving bordello at 408 Cactus (GPS 32.77977, -108.15866).

"You either do things for love or money," Millie told a reporter before she died. "I sure didn't do what I did for love."

But she knew romance. As a young woman, she married and divorced twice, and then in 1950, Millie married World War II veteran James Cusey, who owned a local ranch and construction business. They were married 41 years before James' death in 1991. Millie died two years later at age 87, and they are buried together.

Today, an assisted-living facility in Silver City is named for Millie – right next door to the post office built on the site of her local bordellos.

A SLIPPERY GANGSTER
Springer
The former Citizens State Bank was at 400 Maxwell Avenue, or GPS 36.361207, -104.595865. The original building is gone, but a new bank sits on the spot.

Big Bob Brady (1902-1934) was a B-List gangster in the Depression, but he could draw a crowd in the end.

In October 1932, Brady and cohort Frank Philpot held up the Citizens State Bank in Springer and got away with $5,000.

By all rights, the career criminal Brady should have been in prison. He had been arrested in the parking lot of the Carlsbad Caverns (GPS 32.177014, -104.441376) in 1931 while on the lam from an Oklahoma bank robbery. While jailed, he tried to escape and was wounded by a bullet in the head, disfiguring his face for the rest of his life. But he was undeterred: Soon after he recovered, he escaped from an Oklahoma prison and returned to robbing banks, killing at least one deputy. Although not quite as famous as Dillinger or Bonnie & Clyde, Brady was wanted in four different states.

In 1933, Brady was again wounded in a shootout in Tucumcari and hovered near death. But *again* he recovered and went back to prison—and *again* he escaped.

In 1934, after a seven-month crime spree, police ran Brady to ground on a Kansas farm, where he was killed in a shootout. Before Brady was buried in Rosedale Cemetery in Ada, Oklahoma, some 2,500 mourners (and curious onlookers) visited his body in the mortuary.

A MISSING MASTERPIECE
Santa Fe
The crime scene is the New Mexico Museum of Fine Arts, 107 West Palace Avenue, at GPS 35.688107, -105.939161.

Georgia O'Keeffe (1887-1986) had an eye for the enchantment in New Mexico's landscape. The American master not only painted it, she lived in it.

Among her earliest Southwestern works was "Special No. 21 (Palo Duro Canyon)," a small oil-on-board painting that she created in 1916 or 1917. It was displayed in her first solo art show in Manhattan, before she blossomed into one of the most significant modern artists of the 20th century. After O'Keeffe died, her estate donated "Special No. 21" to Santa Fe's Museum of Fine Arts.

In 2003, the painting—now worth nearly $1 million—was stolen off the museum's wall. It had been part of an exhibit featuring other notable modernists, such as Pablo Picasso and Andy Warhol.

O'Keeffe is one of New Mexico's most beloved figures. Between 1929 and 1949, she spent part of every year painting in New Mexico. After her famous photographer husband Alfred Stieglitz died in 1949, she moved permanently to New Mexico, restoring a dilapidated compound in Abiquiu (GPS 36.208066, -106.317569). She split her time between the Abiquiu studio and her sprawling Ghost Ranch summer home (GPS 36.324996, -106.50519) until 1984, when she moved to Santa Fe two years before her death at age ninety-eight.

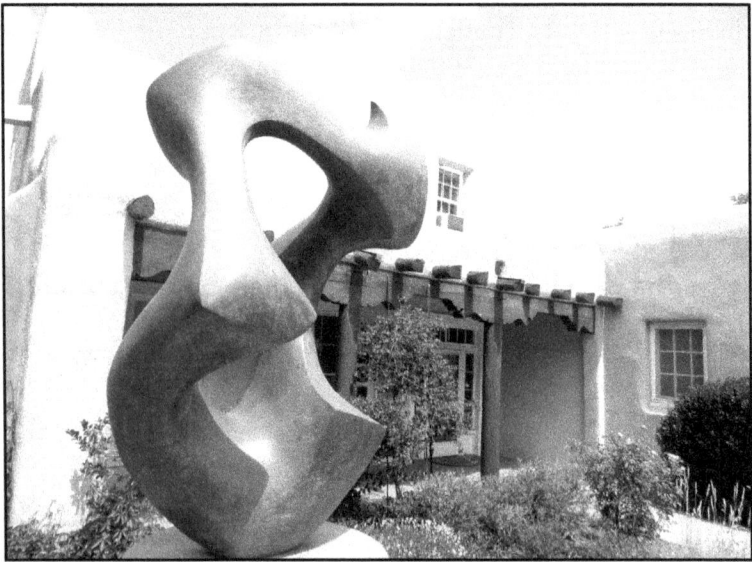

'Special No. 21 (Palo Duro Canyon)' was stolen from the NM Museum of Art and has never been recovered.

Her ashes were scattered over her beloved Pedernal Mountain (GPS 36.16, -106.501389), which appeared in many of her paintings. And her paintings were scattered all over the world in the most prestigious museums and private collections, literally worth hundreds of millions and prime targets for art thieves.

Within months of the theft, New Mexico state police had arrested William Crumpton, a security guard at Santa Fe's private O'Keeffe Museum (217 Johnson Street, GPS 35.689158, -105.941111). Crumpton admitted staging a fake burglary in order to pilfer $14,000 in cash and a different O'Keeffe artwork, her "Red Canna" oil painting, which was recovered undamaged in the museum. He also confessed to stealing $8,000 in cash from the county treasurer's office during a series of local burglaries.

Did Crumpton steal "Special No. 21," too? Under questioning, the feckless Crumpton confessed to playing a role in the theft of "Special No. 21" but provided no significant details.

Then he recanted.

Crumpton was still convicted in the abortive "Red Canna" heist and several downtown burglaries but never charged with the "Special No. 21" theft. He died in 2007 shortly after his release from jail.

O'Keeffe's "Special No. 21 (Palo Duro Canyon)" has never been recovered.

A MYSTERY MASTER
Santa Fe
Santa Fe National Cemetery is at 501 North Guadalupe Street. Author Tony Hillerman's grave is in Section 20, Site 1587, or GPS 35.70209, -105.94530.

Bestselling mystery writer Tony Hillerman (1925-2008) wrote both thrilling plots and brilliant portraits of New Mexican life in eighteen novels featuring Navajo cops Joe Leaphorn and Jim Chee. A newspaperman and college professor, he was hailed as one of America's best crime fiction authors, although he wrote a wide variety of other books, including a children's book, writing texts, and a 2001 autobiography, *Seldom Disappointed.* A decorated combat veteran of World War II, Hillerman died of a heart attack at age eighty-three.

Also in Santa Fe National Cemetery:

- **Charles Bent** (1789-1847) was a prominent mountain man and fur trader who became New Mexico's first territorial governor and a prosperous merchant in Taos. But not everyone was happy when the US took control of the New Mexico territory from Mexico. In 1847, an angry mob of insurgent Mexicans and Pueblo Indians attacked his Taos home (117 Bent Street, GPS 36.408616, -105.573427) and killed him. The house still exists as a museum and art gallery. Bent was originally buried in Santa Fe's old Masonic Cemetery and was among forty-seven bodies moved in 1895 to the new national cemetery. He's in Section C, Site 500 (GPS 35.69535, -105.94882).

- **George Bascom** (1837-1862) was a Union officer in the Civil War who helped trigger the bloody Apache Wars in New Mexico and Arizona, which would last twenty-four years. Bascom was killed by a Confederate bullet in New Mexico's Battle of Valverde in 1852 and buried in Fort Craig; the fort's graveyard was moved to the national cemetery in 1885, but Bascom's remains were unidentifiable, and he's believed to be among the unknown soldiers in Section I (GPS 35.695342, -105.948603). *For more details, see "Mickey Free, Scout" (Arizona).*

THE SPY WHO DISAPPEARED
Santa Fe
Edward Lee Howard's home was at 108 Verano Loop in the Santa Fe suburb of El Dorado, or GPS 35.546763, -105.920826.

After a stint with the Peace Corps, Edward Lee Howard (1951-2002) yearned for more adventure, so he applied to the Central Intelligence Agency. He admitted in his application that he was a moderate drinker and had used a smorgasbord of drugs, including LSD, cocaine and hashish, but the CIA thought his education, overseas experience and gun expertise made him a good prospect. So Howard and his wife were hired as fledgling spooks.

After his training, Howard was prepped for an assignment to Moscow. But shortly before he shipped out, Howard admitted in a polygraph examination that his drinking was more than moderate, he was still using hard drugs, and he occasionally shoplifted. So the CIA forced him to resign in 1983.

The Company helped Howard get a state job in New Mexico, but the ex-spy fumed bitterly. In 1984, he admitted to his former bosses that he'd considered selling CIA secrets to the Soviets but, in fact, he already was.

Then in 1985, a Soviet KGB defector identified Howard as an agent code-named "Robert" who was selling the names of US operatives in the USSR.

While the FBI staked out Howard's house in El Dorado, he made plans to defect to the Soviet Union.

On September 20, 1985, Howard boldly approached one of his FBI watchers and said he was ready to confess but wanted to get a lawyer first. So far, the feds didn't have enough evidence to arrest Howard, so all they could do was keep him under surveillance while they built their case.

OUTLAW NEW MEXICO

CIA turncoat Edward Lee Howard lived in this suburban house at the time he fled to the Soviet Union in 1985.

The next day, Howard's wife drove him to dinner. On the way home, Howard bailed out of the moving car at a blind corner, and his wife propped up a wigged dummy in the passenger seat to fool their FBI pursuers. Back home that night, she called their family doctor's answering machine and played a pre-recorded message by Howard to deceive FBI wiretappers.

A day later, Howard walked into the Soviet Embassy in Helsinki and became the only known US spy to have successfully defected to the Soviet Union. His treachery led to the near-complete collapse of the American spy network in Moscow, resulting in several arrests and executions. The defection also effectively concealed the activities of two other spies, the CIA's Aldrich Ames and FBI's Robert Hanssen, whose ongoing damage was misattributed to Howard.

The KGB gave Howard a modest monthly allowance, a house, and a *dacha*, or country villa. His wife and son occasionally visited and even lived in Europe for a time to be close to Howard. In 1995, he wrote a book, *Safe House: The Compelling Memoirs of the Only CIA Spy to Seek Asylum in Russia*, describing his exploits.

In 2002, the Russians revealed Howard had died of a broken neck suffered in a fall at his *dacha*. His body was reportedly cremated, but the death was never independently verified.

For more about these major spy scandals, see "The Crime Buff's Guide to Outlaw Washington DC"

OUTLAW SAM KETCHUM'S GRAVE
Santa Fe
The Odd Fellows Cemetery is at 1125 Cerrillos Road. The grave is in an untidy corner of the westernmost section of this graveyard, at GPS 35.67402, -105.95987.

With his younger brother Tom, Sam Ketchum made his mark on outlaw history alongside many of the Old West's most infamous badmen.

When honest cowboy work grew too tedious for Sam and Tom, they turned to crime. They began robbing trains, mercantiles, and post offices. When they formed their own gang, they were joined by outlaw friends from Wyoming's Hole in the Wall.

On July 11, 1899, Sam rode into Folsom, New Mexico, with Wild Bunch buddies Kid Curry and Elzy Lay and robbed $50,000 from a train, but a posse trailed him to his Turkey Creek Canyon hideout near Cimarron (GPS 36.521670, -104.982220). In the ensuing shootout, Sam was wounded, and Sheriff Edward Farr was killed. (Farr was buried in the Masonic Cemetery in Walsenburg, Colorado.)

The mortally wounded Sam was taken to the territorial prison in Santa Fe (no longer existing near St. Francis and Cordova roads, GPS 35.673959, -105.954149), where he died on July 24.

He was buried in a parched plot outside the Odd Fellows Cemetery fence. His modern headstone bears the epitaph "Cowboy, Husband, Father & Outlaw."

In 1901, little brother Tom "Black Jack" Ketchum was hanged as a train robber in Clayton. Because of a hangman's miscalculation, Tom was decapitated as he fell through the gallows' trap door.

See also New Mexico Territorial Prison (Santa Fe) and "Black Jack Loses His Head" (Clayton)

Infamous outlaw Sam Ketchum died in custody after being wounded in a train hold-up. He's buried in a desolate corner of Santa Fe's Odd Fellows Cemetery.

NEW MEXICO TERRITORIAL PRISON
Santa Fe
This historic prison no longer exists but was on state property at the southwest corner of St. Francis and Cordova road, at GPS 35.673959, -105.954149.

Before the territory of New Mexico built any other official buildings, it built a prison. The territorial prison opened in 1885 and served its guests until it was razed in 1956 to make room for more modern government buildings.

To address pitiful conditions at most of New Mexico's county jails, the US Congress gave the territory $20,000 in 1853 for a new 108-cell prison. The money ran out before the building was finished, and it sat unfinished for another thirty years until territorial legislators kicked in $150,000 to finish the work.

During its eighty-year history, the territorial (then later state) prison housed some of the biggest names in Western crime, such as Billy the Kid, train robber Sam Ketchum (who died there), and Wild Bunch co-founder Elzy Lay.

In 1929, a bootlegger named George Kelly was busted smuggling booze into an Indian reservation and was imprisoned here. When he got out, he skedaddled to Tulsa and started plotting bigger crimes that would earn him his more famous nickname, "Machine Gun" Kelly.

In 1956, a new state penitentiary was opened southeast of Santa Fe.

See also "Yuma Territorial Prison" (Outlaw Arizona)

DEATH CHAMBER
Santa Fe

New Mexico's mothballed death chamber is in the Level 6 Supermax unit of the New Mexico State Penitentiary, 10 miles southwest of the city, GPS 35.568350, -106.068692. Access is restricted.

A year after New Mexico became America's forty-seventh state in 1912, it began executing outlaws. In more than a century since then, twenty-eight killers have been hanged, gassed, electrocuted, or injected with lethal drugs by state executioners. (Before 1912, all condemned inmates were executed by county sheriffs.)

It all started with a spectacle. In April 1913, killers Ivory Frazer and Francisco Granado—convicted in unrelated crimes—were hanged simultaneously at sunrise outside the Socorro County Jail.

Justice was swift in those days. In 1916, the state hanged six Mexican nationals captured during Pancho Villa's deadly raid on Columbus two months before. Eighteen Americans and seventy-three Villistas were killed in the terrorist attack. One of those Villistas, Juan Sanchez, was cut down from the gallows but started breathing again. His second hanging was more successful.

In all, nineteen men were hanged.

In 1933, New Mexico abandoned the gallows in favor of the electric chair, in which seven murderers died.

The gas chamber was a short-lived experiment for New Mexico. In 1960, homicidal hitchhiker David Cooper Nelson winked at reporters before becoming the first and last to die in New Mexico's gas chamber, which is now stored in the Old Main section of the Penitentiary of New Mexico. It would be forty-one years before the state executed another killer.

Lethal injection became the state's preferred execution method in 1980, after the US Supreme Court's long moratorium on capital punishment. But New Mexico was in no hurry. The day before leaving office in 1986, Governor Tony Anaya commuted the sentences of all death row inmates in New Mexico.

But few people disagreed about the worthiness of New Mexico's last dead man walking.

Terry Clark had raped and murdered a 9-year-old Artesia girl, Dena Lynn Gore, in 1986—only a year after he was convicted of raping another little girl. His earlier victim was among the witnesses who watched Clark executed in 2001 by lethal injection.

But Clark left one more mystery with his last words. "Fifteen minutes," is all he said.

New Mexico abolished capital punishment in 2009, but two convicted killers remain on death row because their crimes happened before 2009.

See also "A Child Murder" (Artesia) and "The Columbus Raid" (Columbus)

DEADLY PENITENTIARY RIOT
Santa Fe
The empty Old Main Prison is still part of the penitentiary's modernized complex about ten miles southwest of the capital, at GPS 35.566521, -106.064831.

In the graveyard hour after midnight on February 2, 1980, prison inmates drunk on secretly brewed prison hooch engulfed four startled guards and sparked one of the bloodiest prison riots in American history.

Over the next thirty-six hours, rioters held twelve guards hostage, took complete control of the prison's communications center, rampaged through the cellblocks, and exacted savage revenge in a bloody spree of beatings, rapes, and stabbings. Thirty-three inmates were killed and almost a hundred grievously wounded in the barbaric chaos.

Years of anger had erupted in a furious explosion. The prison was overcrowded, and programs that had averted boredom and trouble had been cut. And guards exerted control over misbehaving inmates with a "snitch game," where they threatened to leak their names as informants. Gangs grew more powerful. Security had grown complacent. The prison had become even more hellish than prison should be.

Once they controlled the prison, inmates were merciless in their destruction. They used blowtorches to cut into Cellblock Four, the protective custody wing where "execution squads" tortured, dismembered and decapitated anyone they felt was a snitch. In one grisly case, they held a blowtorch to an inmate's face until his head exploded.

Responding to inmates' demands, the governor allowed a TV cameraman to go inside for a televised news conference after inmates had allowed the most injured guards go free.

Finally, the inmates surrendered after thirty-six tense hours, and New Mexico National Guardsmen retook the prison.

A few inmates were prosecuted, but most of the riot's worst crimes went unpunished. No state officials were implicated in any wrongdoing. The uprising was one of the deadliest in US history, second only to the 1971 Attica Prison riot.

Author Roger Morris' 1988 book, *The Devil's Butcher Shop,* offers an unblinking account of the causes and the horrors of the uprising.

Last used in 1998, the old prison is little changed since the riot, although some artifact displays have been added. Today, it's frequently rented to Hollywood film and TV producers for prison scenes.

A-BOMB SPIES
Santa Fe

The historic Castillo Street Bridge over the Santa Fe River was replaced by a modern bridge at Paseo de Peralta and East Alameda, or GPS 35.684238, -105.933967.

On the bright-hot afternoon of June 2, 1945, a beat-up gray Buick sedan approached the Castillo Street Bridge, where a short, plump man waited nervously, out of place in his raincoat and fedora.

The Buick stopped and the man got in. It rolled slowly across the bridge and down the dirt road, not far, to a dusty lane that ended at a gate. It stopped.

The driver was slender and stern, and he spoke with a German accent. The two men talked seriously for a moment before the driver handed his passenger a fat manila envelope.

In that moment, on a bright New Mexico afternoon, history changed.

That envelope contained the primary design of the atomic bomb.

Dr. Klaus Fuchs was the primary physicist on the super-secret Manhattan Project in nearby Los Alamos. His contact was Harry Gold, an unemployed American chemist and Soviet courier code-named "Raymond."

A month later, the US tested the first atomic bomb in the New Mexico desert at White Sands (GPS 33.677321, -106.475567). Fuchs was among the scientists who watched, knowing that he had already set in motion a worldwide arms race even before the first nuclear bomb had exploded.

And a month after that test, the first atomic bombs were dropped on Hiroshima and Nagasaki, ending World War II and starting a new kind of war.

New Mexico's role in the birth of the atomic bomb and the nuclear age is huge. Not only was the first device developed in the secluded hills of Los Alamos where secrets were easier to keep, and tested in the lonely desert, but Santa Fe and Albuquerque were also scenes in the science and intrigue.

A back room in Sena Plaza between 107 and 109 East Palace Avenue (GPS 35.687700, -105.957035) was the Manhattan Project's Santa Fe headquarters during World War II. This was the clandestine gateway to Los Alamos, where scientists and workers received strict instructions, travel and living arrangements.

Dr. Robert Oppenheimer led the Manhattan Project, a sprawling collection of buildings and mysterious activities on "The Hill." Oppenheimer lived at 1967 Peach Street (GPS 35.0884004, -106.301806), in a neighborhood known as Bathtub Row where many of the key scientists lived, including Fuchs. History still debates whether other scientists knew about the nuclear espionage.

On September 18, Gold returned to New Mexico. He stayed with another Los Alamos worker, David Greenglass, in a second-floor apartment at 209 High Street NE in Albuquerque (Apartment No. 4, at GPS 35.084449, -106.639903), where he collected more information for his Soviet handlers. Greenglass had been recruited into the spy game by his wife Ruth, who had herself been recruited by her sister Ethel Rosenberg.

The next night, Fuchs and Gold met again in Santa Fe, this time in a church. This time, Fuchs passed along data about uranium and plutonium production before Gold went back to New York with a suitcase full of secrets.

It all came unraveled after the Soviets tested their first A-bomb in 1949. American spies had found some of Fuchs' work in secret Russian reports, and the Soviets' new bomb looked suspiciously like one Fuchs had designed in the Manhattan Project.

Then working in London, Fuchs readily confessed to his crimes. He led investigators to Gold, who led them to the Greenglasses, who led them to Ethel and Julius Rosenberg, the ringleaders.

Fuchs went to British prison but was released in a Soviet prisoner exchange in 1959. He died a Soviet citizen in 1988.

Gold also went to prison and was paroled in 1966. He died in 1972 and is buried at Har Nebo Cemetery, 6001 Oxford Avenue, The Great Northwest, Pennsylvania. Gold's grave is in Section O, six rows back from the sign, at GPS 40.03980, -75.08570.

Greenglass spent a few years in prison and was released. At last report, he was living on the East Coast.

Julius and Ethel Rosenberg were tried and executed in 1953. They were buried together in Wellwood Cemetery in Farmingdale, New York. Their graves are in Block 5, Row G at GPS 40.736733, -73.396868.

Today, the Albuquerque boarding house where Gold and Greenglass met is the Spy House bed and breakfast. Rooms are named after the spies Gold, Greenglass, and Rosenberg.

New Mexico's rich spy history is explored in *A Spy's Guide to Santa Fe and Albuquerque* (2011) by former CIA agent E.B. Held.

HISTORY ON DISPLAY
Santa Fe
The New Mexico History Museum/Palace of the Governors is at 113 Lincoln Avenue, or GPS 35.688288, -105.938474. 10-5 Tues-Sun. Admission charged.

Over the past hundred years, the State of New Mexico has collected some fascinating artifacts of its crime history, including:

- Billy the Kid's spurs, ca. 1870s
- Original letters Billy the Kid wrote to Lew Wallace seeking a pardon, 1879 and 1881
- Teresina Bent's diary describing how she witnessed the murder of her father, Gov. Charles Bent, during the 1847 Taos Rebellion
- A rifle seized from activist Reies Tijerina after his 1967 shootout at the Tierra Amarilla courthouse
- A silver *peineta* (hair ornament) on loan from the Albuquerque Museum and a pewter goblet on loan from the Museum of Spanish Colonial Art, both owned by legendary saloon operator and madam Dona Tules
- A 1915 Seth Thomas wall clock from the railway station, pierced front and back by a bullet during Pancho Villa's raid on Columbus, NM (with a bullet hole at 6 o'clock and hands stopped at 4:11)
- Pancho Villa's death mask (with a bullet hole in the forehead)
- A Villista revolver from the Columbus raid
- Villa's 1916 letter to Emiliano Zapata warning him that they shared a common enemy: The United States

TWO CASES, ONE JUDGE
Santa Fe
Fairview Cemetery is on the west side of the intersection of Cerillos Road and Cordova Road. The grave is in Section B, Plot 189, at GPS 35.675579, -105.958704.

Judge Frank W. Parker (1860-1932) was one of New Mexico's most prominent legal figures and presided over two high-profile criminal trials with questionable verdicts.

A former boomtown lawyer, he was a friend of renowned (and corrupt) defense attorney Albert B. Fall and openly disliked Sheriff Pat Garrett.

As territorial judge, Parker sat on the 1899 trial of ranchers Oliver Lee and Jim Gililland for the presumed murder of lawyer Albert Jennings Fountain and his young son, who had disappeared three years before. Both had been arrested by Pat Garrett—and defended by Albert Fall. The trial made national news, but the two accused killers were ultimately acquitted.

Ten years later, Parker sat on the 1909 murder trial of Wayne Brazel, who'd already confessed to killing Pat Garrett. Brazel was represented by Fall and, again, the killer walked free, despite his admissions. Suspicions abound that Garrett's murder was really a conspiracy by his enemies in the earlier Fountain case.

Always a political animal, Parker eventually became a New Mexico Supreme Court justice.

ESCAPE BY HELICOPTER
Santa Fe
The current Penitentiary of New Mexico is at GPS 35.566521, -106.064831.

On July 11, 1988, real estate developer Beverly Shoemaker hired El Paso helicopter pilot Charles Bella to take her up to scout some property near Santa Fe.

Shoemaker was a big woman and sat in the rear seat, telling Bella where to fly. But as they neared the airspace over the Penitentiary of New Mexico, Shoemaker pulled out a .357 Magnum and shoved its barrel against the pilot's head.

She was not a real estate developer at all, but a desperate woman in love with a killer inside the prison.

And this was going to be a prison break worthy of Hollywood.

Shoemaker ordered Bella to land in the prison yard, where three prisoners would quickly board. He protested, saying the chopper wouldn't be able to carry all of them safely, but she was adamant.

So with a gun at his head, Bella set his helicopter down near the prison baseball field and three inmates jumped aboard. One of them handcuffed Bella to the craft and they flew south, with two US Customs Blackhawks in pursuit.

After a short time in the air, the inmates ordered Bella to land at Mid-Valley Airpark in Los Lunas (GPS 34.759252, -106.744579), south of Albuquerque, where Shoemaker and two of the inmates fled. But before federal agents could secure the helicopter, a third inmate—also a killer—ordered Bella at gunpoint to take off again. After a wild, fifty-minute chase in the air, Bella and the inmate were arrested at Albuquerque International Sunport (GPS 35.046925, -106.617170). Shoemaker and the other two escapees were also caught and convicted in the escape.

Bella was charged as a conspirator in the escape. Two of the escapees said Bella had always been part of the plan, but Shoemaker testified Bella—who'd passed three polygraph tests—was an innocent abductee. The pilot was acquitted after a ten-day trial. Celebrity attorney F. Lee Bailey was his lawyer.

PROSE OR PORN?
Taos

The D.H. Lawrence Memorial is on his Taos-area ranch, at GPS 36.582935, -105.593705. Traveling north of Taos on New Mexico 522, a rutted county road (B-009) leads five miles to the property. Signage is unpredictable.

There's a little outlaw in every author. For some, the law actually gets involved.

D.H. Lawrence (1885-1930) saw that sensuality and justice were entangled concepts. But he never expected them to collide head-on.

The British author of 1920s classics such as *Sons and Lovers* and *Women in Love* found personal solace in a northern New Mexico ranch even as his most famous (or infamous) novel was taking shape in his mind.

In the early 1920s, Lawrence and his wife Frieda visited Taos often. In 1924, wealthy arts patron Mabel Dodge Luhan gave the Lawrences the 160-acre Kiowa Ranch on Lobo Mountain near Taos. Its isolation and quiet soothed Lawrence, and he wrote some of his best poetry and short stories while holed up in the solitude.

When doctors diagnosed Lawrence with tuberculosis, he and Frieda moved to Italy (although they kept the ranch).

In late 1929, Lawrence finished his masterwork, *Lady Chatterley's Lover.* It describes in delicious detail the

Author D.H. Lawrence's ashes are said to be mixed into the concrete used to build this altar in a small memorial on his ranch near Taos.

love affair between a wealthy, married woman and a gamekeeper who works on her indifferent husband's estate. Its explicit descriptions of sex, erotic language, and carnal themes made it immediately controversial.

The US officially banned it as obscene in 1928. Customs officials seized Lawrence's self-published copies at the border, and the Postal Service not only confiscated mailed copies, but also *orders* for copies. *Lady Chatterley's Lover* remained a forbidden work in America (and many other countries) for thirty years, until a landmark obscenity trial in 1959 allowed it to be published and sold.

Lawrence never returned to New Mexico, at least while he was alive. He died and was buried in France in 1930.

But Frieda returned to live at the ranch with a new husband. In 1934, she made an odd request: She wanted Lawrence's remains to be returned to New Mexico, where she was building a small, white-plastered shrine to his memory.

So Lawrence's corpse was reportedly exhumed, cremated in France, and then the ashes shipped to Taos, where Frieda supposedly mixed them into the mortar for a small altar in her late husband's memorial. Some of Lawrence's friends and admirers were appalled, including Mabel Dodge Luhan, who called Frieda's memorial "that outhouse of a shrine."

Frieda was buried there when she died in 1956.

Among the pilgrims who've paid their respects at Lawrence's memorial are playwright Tennessee Williams, novelist Iris Murdoch, and artist Georgia O'Keeffe, whose vivid painting "The Lawrence Tree" captures a view from the trunk of a contorted pine in front of the author's cabin, just down the hill.

In the end, D.H. Lawrence's artistic transgressions were forgiven, or at least forgotten. Today, nearly a century later, Lawrence is considered a twentieth-century literary master, and *Lady Chatterley's Lover* is available at every bookstore.

MAD DOGS AND AN ENGLISHMAN
Taos

The crime scene is now a café at 133 Paseo del Pueblo Norte, at GPS 36.40834, -105.57243.

Arthur Manby (1869-1929) was an eccentric, unscrupulous Brit, supposedly a bad-boy son whose wealthy family sent him away with a monthly stipend as long as he never came home. He lived in a fortified adobe hacienda, wore English riding pants and a floppy hat, and slung a pistol at his waist.

Rumors about possibly illegal activities followed him almost as faithfully as the fearsome, ugly dog at his side. Most folks avoided him—and he liked it that way.

On July 3, 1929, a US deputy marshal came to Manby's house to serve papers. When nobody answered, the deputy killed Manby's ferocious guard dogs and leaped over the wall. Inside, he found Manby dead on an Army cot, his head missing. The deputy soon found the Englishman's skull, which had been gnawed clean by one of his hungry dogs.

The coroner ruled Manby died of natural causes, but rumors swirled that he'd been murdered for his money. Some even believe the death had been staged and that Manby fled the country. His ghost is said to still haunt the historic house.

Manby was buried near the Kit Carson Cemetery, on Dragoon Lane near downtown Taos. His grave is just a few feet beyond the fence at GPS 36.40860, -105.56926.

TIERRA AMARILLA SHOOTOUT
Tierra Amarilla
The Tierra Amarilla courthouse is at 7 Main Street, or GPS 36.698429, -106.552078.

Reies Lopez Tijerina (b. 1926) was an itinerant preacher from Texas. In the 1950s, he led a small band of followers into the Arizona desert to establish a secluded colony where his followers lived in underground houses so they could educate their children, safely shielded from the influence of state-run schools.

In 1957, after Arizona threatened legal action to force the colony's children into public school—and after Tijerina fled prosecution for his role in a botched jailbreak—he and his followers disappeared into northern New Mexico, where he became obsessed with what he saw as the unjust theft of old Mexican land grants by Anglo powerbrokers and politicians.

Then the fugitive Tijerina had a mystical dream. He saw frozen horses melting in the sun. He interpreted it as a message from God telling him to free the frozen horses— take back the old Mexican land grants from the Anglo government and corporations—and give them back to their heirs.

It was true that over more than a century, large tracts of Mexican land given to early settlers had been bought or seized by powerful people, like the Santa Fe Ring's Thomas B. Catron and other politicians, who often operated on the fringes of legality.

But Tijerina's claims were based more on emotion and ethnic pride than legal evidence. They resonated at a time when the civil rights movement was dominating headlines across the US.

In 1963, Tijerina founded the grassroots protest group Alianza Federal de Mercedes (Federal Alliance of Land Grants). For several years, they peacefully protested in marches across New Mexico, but the small, vocal group grew impatient.

On June 5, 1967, Tijerina led about twenty armed men into the Rio Arriba County Courthouse in Tierra Amarilla, attempting a citizen's arrest of the district attorney (who wasn't there). In the angry chaos, a state police officer and a jailer were shot and wounded as Tijerina's raiders took a reporter and a sheriff's deputy hostage.

Eventually, the New Mexico National Guard, FBI, and New Mexico State Police caught up to Tijerina, and the hostages were freed. Tijerina was convicted of kidnapping and armed assault and sentenced to three years in prison.

Undeterred by prison, Tijerina continued his fight, eventually taking it to Washington, D.C. On June 23, 1969, the day Warren Burger was sworn in as Chief Justice, Tijerina planned to place him under citizen's arrest, but he had to flee the Capitol Building to avoid arrest.

After another federal prison stretch related to the courthouse raid (when his cellmate was mob informer Joe Valachi) and time in a mental hospital, Tijerina emerged back into the free world, where he remains an active voice on southwestern land issues.

TWICE HANGED
Tinnie
The killer's grave is in a field beside the Silver Dollar restaurant, GPS 33.36970, -105.22188 on private property.

In 1875, a hired gun named William Wilson murdered a well-liked local rancher, Robert Casey. It was one of the earliest killings in the bloody Lincoln County War.

Wilson was convicted and sentenced to hang. On the appointed day, he shook hands with onlookers and mounted the scaffold in front of the old Lincoln County Courthouse (now known as the *Convento* at GPS 33.49186, -105.38589). In a few moments, he dropped through the trap door and dangled at the end of his rope for almost ten minutes before the hangman cut him down and laid his body in a pine coffin.

Soon, a Mexican woman in the crowd screamed, "The dead has come to life!"

Wilson had begun breathing.

The hangman quickly looped the noose around Wilson's neck again and hoisted him into the air. This time they waited a full twenty minutes before they packed him up for burial.

Wilson was buried in an unmarked grave in a field near Tinnie, fifteen miles southeast of Lincoln.

Casey was buried in his family cemetery near Picacho (GPS 33.36774, -105.18457)

See also the Billy the Kid Chapter.

THE TOY BOX KILLER
Truth or Consequences/Elephant Butte
The serial killer's trailer was at 513 Bass Road, or GPS 33.206601, -107.213010. This is private property.

David Parker Ray (1939-2002) grew up shy, abused, and repressed. He was painfully inept around women, which might be why he married and divorced four times in his life.

Or maybe there was something else. Possibly while still a teenager in the 1950s, Ray might have begun abducting, raping and torturing young women. Sometimes with an accomplice, sometimes alone, Ray often lured hookers to his home, where he'd get sexual gratification by inflicting great pain. He freed many of them, but only after taking clothing or jewelry as little trophies.

Eventually, the mechanic built a $100,000 torture chamber from an old, twenty-foot trailer and called it his "Toy Box." He filled it with sex toys, surgical instruments, chains, saws, straps, leg-spreader bars, syringes, audio and video equipment, a homemade coffin, and a sadistic electrical rack. A mirror on the ceiling meant his victims could see everything he was doing to them.

One of his accomplices, a girlfriend named Cindy Hendy, later claimed some women died during the torture or were slain in the cruel orgy. Those unfortunates were dismembered and their pieces buried, dumped in the nearby Elephant Butte Lake, or tossed in ravines for varmints.

Ray was finally arrested in 1999, when one of his victims escaped a three-day torture session and ran naked down the road wearing only chains and a slave collar. The sensational story drew national headlines, and many of Ray's surviving victims came forward with harrowing

How many women were imprisoned and tortured in David Ray's "toy box" near Elephant Butte? Nobody knows.

tales, many saying Ray had drugged them into believing the horrors were just nightmares.

FBI agents scoured Ray's property and the adjacent lake but found no human remains.

Before a series of trials was to start, Ray pleaded guilty to abducting and torturing three women at his Elephant Butte trailer. He avoided the death penalty and got 224 years in prison. Accomplice Hendy got thirty-six years.

He also claimed that he had abducted as many as forty women in several states, but to date, no human remains have been connected to him.

On May 28, 2002, Ray was about to be interrogated by New Mexico State Police about his crimes when he died of a heart attack

During their searches of Ray's "Toy Box," investigators found hundreds of items they believe Ray kept as trophies of his victims. The FBI has posted photos of these items online in hopes someone can identify their owners. You can search for them at *www.fbi.gov/news*.

ALBERT FOUNTAIN VANISHES
Near White Sands
A historical sign marks the spot where Fountain and his eight-year-old son were last seen alive, at Milepost 178 on US 70, at GPS 32.517652, -106.375423.

In the 1890s, rustlers were running amok in southern New Mexico and cattle barons were angry. They hired legislator and respected lawyer Albert Jennings Fountain of Mesilla to prosecute gangs of cattle thieves who were stealing thousands of head.

In January 1896, he successfully indicted small rancher Oliver M. Lee and his gang of cowboys for rustling. A few days later, on February 1, Fountain and his eight-year-old son Henry set out by buckboard toward their Mesilla home.

Along the way, they disappeared forever. The buckboard was found later, but not the father and son.

Suspicion immediately fell on Oliver Lee, but it was two years before legendary Sheriff Pat Garrett could gather enough evidence to arrest him and two of his cowboys, Jim Gililland and William McNew—who hired prominent lawyer (and arch-nemesis of Albert Jennings Fountain) Albert B. Fall.

But their prosecutor, Thomas B. Catron, was equally skilled, and the case suddenly garnered national headlines as a clash of legal titans.

Charges against McNew were eventually dropped, so Lee and Gililland faced the jury together for the presumed first-degree murder of little Henry Fountain. The courtroom drama was thick but in the end, the jury took only eight minutes to acquit Lee and Gililland.

Many alternative theories have arisen, including outlaw Sam Ketchum's story that he watched his own brother, the cold-blooded bandit Tom "Black Jack" Ketchum, kill the Fountains. Nevertheless, to this day,

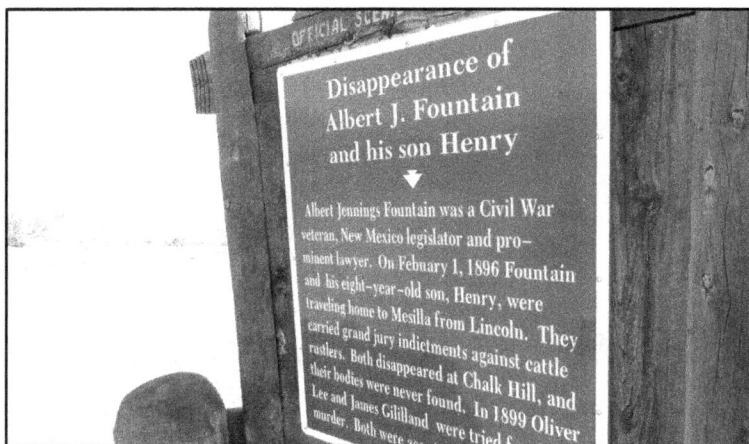

Albert Fountain and his son have never been found.

nobody has ever been convicted of the Fountain killings.

Although Albert and Henry's bodies were never found, a cenotaph was erected in their memory at Las Cruces' Masonic Cemetery, 760 South Compress Road, at Section A, Block 12, or GPS 32.29987, -106.78404.

Accused killer Oliver M. Lee (1865-1941) was more popular than ever after his acquittal. He became a respected state senator and died an old man. He's buried in Alamogordo's Monte Vista Cemetery, 1590 East First Street at GPS 32.88962, -105.94341.

His ranch became the Oliver Lee State Park, 409 Dog Canyon Road, Alamogordo (GPS 32.746329, -105.916107).

Cohort James R. Gililland (1874-1946) also lived to old age. He was buried in the Mason's Row at Tularosa's Fairview Cemetery at GPS 33.082456, -106.018411.

Their conniving defender, Albert Fall (1861-1944), became Secretary of the Interior, where he was convicted of corruption in the infamous Teapot Dome Scandal. He died impoverished. He's buried in El Paso's Evergreen Alameda Cemetery, 4371 Alameda Avenue. His grave is in Section K, Lot 211 (GPS 31.77337, -106.44018).

Prosecutor Thomas B. Catron (1840-1921) later became a US senator and was embroiled in his own controversies as part of the infamous Santa Fe Ring. He is buried in an elaborate family mausoleum at Santa Fe's Fairview Cemetery at GPS 35.67517, -105.95870.

Fountain's memory is still alive, too. The Fountain Theatre, built in 1905 by his family, remains open and is still owned by Fountain descendants. The oldest continuously operated theatre in New Mexico is at 2469 Calle de Guadalupe in Mesilla (GPS 32.273713, -106.794548).

II
BILLY THE KID

We know almost nothing of this gypsy photographer, drifting the dusty roads of the territories. Trooping wearily from one far-flung town to another, he'd likely stop his dark-room wagon outside of busy saloons, brothels, maybe even a hanging. He'd mount his big camera, unfurl his backdrops, and hope the word spread before dark that there was a man taking pictures in town.

But the itinerant, nameless lensman who stopped outside Beaver Smith's rough saloon in Fort Sumner, New Mexico, one day in 1880, not only made a two-bit tintype for a young, slightly dopey-looking cowboy who posed stock-still with his Winchester and six-shooter for less than ten seconds.

In less than ten seconds, that unknown photographer captured the most iconic image of the Old West. He also captured a hundred years of light and shadow, myth and illusion, life and death.

He shot Billy the Kid.

When Pat Garrett shot Billy about a year later, Billy's life was over. But this image, roughly the size of a modern-day credit card, gave Billy everlasting life.

Forever, Billy would be this buck-toothed boy, barely a man, in his crumpled sugarloaf sombrero, a scarf and

baggy pants tucked into his boots, his Colt slung loose on his hip, his head cocked smugly—even though the photographer had braced his neck for the long exposure. And only a keen eye would spot the gambler's ring on his pinky finger.

Cameras might not lie, but they can make myths. In the coming century, the fact that the image showed his revolver on his left caused many people—including some filmmakers—to assume Billy was left-handed. In reality, a tintype is a reverse image and Billy wore his pistol on his right side.

But like tintypes themselves, the history of the American West is sharply focused at the center, then grows fuzzier around the edges until it's a complete illusion. So it was with Billy the Kid.

This is the single most recognizable image of the Old West, even more familiar than the Fort Worth portrait of Butch Cassidy's Wild Bunch. It both reflects and defines the period. And it is the only authenticated photograph of a quintessential outlaw who launched a thousand dime novels, poems, plays, songs, headlines, and movies. Did you know Billy the Kid now holds the record for the most films made about any single person in Hollywood history?

His known biography has more holes than his movie victims. Who was his father? When and where was he born? Why did he go wrong? We'll likely never know any of those answers.

Although Billy the Kid claimed he killed twenty-one men – "one for every year of my life" he supposedly boasted in what might also be a dime-novel fabrication—his authenticated death toll is only about half that. More lethal than Butch Cassidy, but a long day's ride behind Jesse James.

And just as this image doesn't tell us everything we should know about William Henry McCarty, neither does history. Much of what we think we know is wrong. Much of his legend is romanticized and corrupted, either willfully or accidentally.

Most likely, Billy was an uncontrollable juvenile delinquent who was a good shot, a trigger-happy twerp who hung out with a bad crowd, an ordinary sociopath. Probably not the faithful, wise, bright, young, and tragic rebel of myth, where he's been portrayed by the heroic likes of Paul Newman, Buster Crabbe, Val Kilmer, Roy Rogers, and Audie Murphy.

The romance obscures our vision. Like Butch Cassidy and Jesse James, some people believe Billy the Kid never died in a blaze of glory, but rather finished out his years as an aged, infirm codger who never committed another crime after his fake death. For all three of those outlaws, that would be unlikely.

But that picture keeps Billy alive. In 2012, the only known image of Henry McCarty sold for $2.3 million, not because it was the last tintype ever made of him, but because of the light and shadow, the myth and illusions, the life and death we call Billy the Kid.

It might be a long time before it fades away.

BILLY THE KID ... AS A KID

If anybody wrote it down, the record hasn't survived history.

William Henry McCarty was probably born in New York City (or Indiana) in 1859. Or 1860. Maybe 1861. He had an older brother Joseph (although Joseph might have been, in fact, younger).

Clearly, little Billy's earliest years are shrouded in mystery and myth.

But by 1866, history starts to notice. Census records show his Irish-born mother Catherine McCarty and two sons living at 199 North East Street in Indianapolis, Indiana. In time, Catherine moves in with a Civil War veteran named William Antrim, and in 1869 Antrim and the McCarty family moved to Kansas, where Catherine ran a laundry and Antrim worked odd jobs as a carpenter, farmhand, and bartender.

In 1872, when young Henry—as they called him to avoid confusion with William Antrim—was on the verge of adolescence, they all moved to Denver to soothe Catherine's tuberculosis, but not for long. By March 1873, they were in Santa Fe, New Mexico, where Catherine McCarty and William Antrim were married in the First Presbyterian Church (208 Grant Avenue, or GPS 35.689885, -105.940440), with Henry and Joseph as witnesses.

But, again, they didn't stay long and soon moved to the mining town of Silver City, New Mexico. They lived in a cabin near the river (very close to a replica now at 201 North Hudson, GPS 32.769833, -108.275439). Catherine's

This replica of Billy's childhood cabin sits near the spot where Billy grew up in Silver City.

tuberculosis was in its final stage, but she quickly started taking boarders, selling baked goods and doing other people's laundry to support the family.

She grew sicker and died in September 1874. She was first buried in the city cemetery, then later moved to Memory Lane Cemetery, east of town on Memory Lane, south of US Route 180. Her grave is in Plot D-E27-14 (GPS 32.78337, -108.25623).

Orphaned as a young teenager, young Henry quickly found himself on his own. He bounced between friends and family, working menial jobs and associating with local ruffians until he was arrested for the first time, less than a year after his mother's death. Accused of stealing some clothing from a Chinese laundry, Henry was tossed in jail, which he managed to escape by climbing up the chimney. Now a fugitive, he lit out for Arizona.

The first of many jail escapes sets young Henry on the outlaw trail. For the rest of his short life, he'll be in the wind.

BILLY'S FIRST KILLING
Bonita, Arizona
The Bonita Store/Atkins Saloon crime scene is one mile northwest of the junction of Arizona 266 and Arizona Industrial School Road, or GPS 32.589659, -109.969344. This structure still exists but is on private property.

A fugitive by age sixteen, Henry McCarty re-invented himself out of necessity.

He fled to Arizona and called himself Kid Antrim. He declared himself a cowboy and drifted from ranch to ranch until 1877, when he hired on as a teamster at the Fort Grant Army Post (now a state prison at GPS 32.622797, -109.946310).

The scrawny, buck-toothed Kid was popular around the camp, even though he had developed a gambling jones and was secretly rustling horses on the side. He also grew increasingly fascinated with dime novels that inflated the exploits of outlaws, none of whom would ever prove as hard to hold as Henry McCarty.

On February 17, 1877, a constable in Globe, Arizona, threw The Kid in jail for stealing a soldier's horse, but later that same day, Billy's cell was found empty.

On March 25, 1877, The Kid was arrested by soldiers for horse theft. Although shackled and locked in the guardhouse, he escaped while his guards attend a camp dance.

One of The Kid's antagonists was a hulking blacksmith named Frank "Windy" Cahill. At the Atkins Saloon on August 17, 1877, Cahill called The Kid a "pimp" and Billy snarled back, insulting Cahill as "a son of a

Bonita Store is the former tavern where Billy killed his first man in a drunken barroom fight in 1877.

bitch."

The brawny blacksmith threw the skinny Kid on the floor and pinned him down. The overmatched Kid panicked. He drew his pistol and shot Cahill, who died the next day.

But Kid Antrim didn't wait for the sheriff. His latest escape took him back to New Mexico, where his outlaw myth—and his own infatuation with it—was about to blossom.

LINCOLN COUNTY WAR ERUPTS
Lincoln, New Mexico
The Tunstall Store is on US 380, the main street through Lincoln, at GPS 33.492831, -105.387061.

Fleeing Arizona, The Kid—now calling himself William Bonney—landed in the little village of Lincoln, New Mexico. He took a job at a cheese factory owned by Doc Scurlock and Charlie Bowdre, who soon introduced him to a band of friends who shared The Kid's felonious spunk.

Late in 1877, Billy and his friends were hired as cowboys by Englishman John Tunstall and prominent lawyer Alexander McSween, who had recently established a ranch, bank and mercantile in the town, much to the dismay of Irishmen Lawrence Murphy and James Dolan, who had held a profitable (and shady) monopoly on Lincoln County's commerce. Animosity simmered.

On February 18, 1878, it boiled over. That morning, Tunstall embarked from his ranch with Billy and four other cowboys to deliver some horses to Lincoln. On the way, they were stopped by a posse of Murphy-Dolan henchmen (GPS 33.363832, -105.436194, a remote site near County Road 9019D, about three miles from a roadside historical marker on US 70 at GPS 33.408967, -105.451883). Tunstall was executed, and the posse rode off before Billy and the others could ride back to help.

Tunstall was buried behind his store (GPS 33.49295, -105.38666). Billy, Scurlock, Bowdre, and their fellow cowboys were quickly deputized by the Lincoln justice of the peace to help solve the crime. But these "Regulators," as they called themselves, were not focused on justice. They wanted vengeance.

The Lincoln County War, one of the Old West's most infamous political and economic clashes, had begun.

Rancher John Tunstall was bushwhacked at a remote spot.

BILLY DRAWS SECOND BLOOD
Lincoln, New Mexico
The Brady-Hindman burial site is about a mile east of Lincoln, at GPS 33.477301, -105.3647421. This is private property.

The Regulators wasted no time wreaking revenge. They trailed and captured Tunstall's suspected killers, who

---

were murdered while "resisting arrest" on the way back to jail.

On April 1, 1878, Billy and five other Regulators ambushed Sheriff William Brady and Deputy George Hindman as they walked down Lincoln's Main Street. The two lawmen were buried side-by-side on Sheriff Brady's ranch east of town.

Billy was slightly wounded, but the Regulators escaped. The cold-blooded assassination was a public relations disaster for the Regulators, who'd been enjoying a fair amount of public support.

BLAZER'S MILL FIGHT
Near Mescalero, New Mexico
A historical marker stands near the former site of Blazer's Mill on US 70 three miles west of Mescalero, at GPS 33.162021, -105.835188.

Three days after the Brady killing, sixteen Regulators hid out at Blazer's Mill, a sawmill, store, and way station some thirty miles southwest of Lincoln.

They were eating when Andrew "Buckshot" Roberts—whom they suspected in Tunstall's murder—accidentally stumbled into the village. When the shooting started, Roberts was wounded in the belly but ran to an adobe building where he barricaded himself inside with a deadly Sharps buffalo rifle.

In the ensuing stand-off, the Regulators' leader, Dick Brewer, was killed. Billy, Scurlock, Bowdre, and a few others were slightly wounded so they retreated, leaving the gutshot Roberts to die in his sniper's nest.

The next day, adversaries Roberts and Brewer were buried side-by-side in the Blazer family cemetery, west of Mescalero at GPS 33.15676, -105.78596. In an ironic twist, Roberts was later proved innocent of any role in Tunstall's murder.

FIVE-DAY WAR
Lincoln, New Mexico
The McSween House once sat on the lot just west of the Tunstall-McSween Store, at GPS 33.492944, -105.387385.

Bad blood persisted for months after the Blazer's Mill fight.

On July 15, 1878, Billy and several Regulators were holed up in Alexander McSween's house in Lincoln when they were suddenly surrounded by dozens of Murphy-Dolan cowboys, led by the new sheriff, George Peppin. The gunfights raged for four days before the raiders set fire to the house and demanded a surrender.

McSween, Billy and the others hastily schemed to escape the flames in the dark, hoping to elude the raiders and Army soldiers who now surrounded them.

Billy, Tom O'Folliard, and Jose Chavez y Chavez successfully escaped, but most of the Regulators and McSween were killed in the furious gunfight that followed.

Alexander McSween (1843-1878) was buried beside his former partner John Tunstall behind their store (GPS 33.49295, -105.38666).

With Tunstall and McSween dead, the Lincoln County War was effectively over. Territorial Governor Lew Wallace granted amnesty to all Regulators except those facing criminal indictments. That was all of them—except Billy Bonney, now wanted for the murder of Sheriff Brady.

ON THE RUN

For months, Billy desperately tried to win amnesty in direct talks with Governor Lew Wallace. In a deal for Billy's testimony before a grand jury about the Murphy-Dolan gang's crimes, Wallace promised to free him after a brief, painless jail stay. But when it became apparent the prosecutor had no intention of letting the killer go free, Billy and Tom O'Folliard fled.

For the next eighteen months, The Kid eluded pursuers, who now included the relentless Sheriff Pat Garrett and soon-to-be-legendary tracker Charles Siringo. He supported himself by rustling, gambling ... and killing.

In November 1880, Billy and a couple other outlaws were resting at the Greathouse-Kuch station (just south of Corona on US 54 between mileposts 168 and 169, or GPS 34.23594, -105.61439) when they were surrounded by local vigilantes. A well-liked blacksmith named Jim Carlyle was killed and Billy was blamed, although some say Carlyle was killed by friendly fire.

During this time, Billy's legend only grew. Outside Beaver Smith's Saloon in Fort Sumner, he paid a traveling photographer twenty-five cents to snap a tintype that became one of the Old West's most iconic images (auctioned in 2011 for $2.3 million).

In December 1880, the editor of the Las Vegas Gazette published an essay in which Henry McCarty, aka Kid Antrim and Billy Bonney, was called "Billy the Kid" for the first time.

CAPTURE ... AND ONE LAST ESCAPE

A few days before Christmas 1880, Billy's life was anything but festive.

With Charlie Bowdre, Billy Wilson, Tom Pickett, and Dave Rudabaugh, he took refuge on the cold, dirt floor of an abandoned rock house at Stinking Springs, about sixteen miles east of Old Fort Sumner (a faint hint of these ruins is on remote, private property at GPS 34.430299, -103.952223).

They were shaken. Sheriff Pat Garrett's posse had surprised them in Fort Sumner a few days before, killing Billy's close friend Tom O'Folliard.

They escaped, but Garrett was unrelenting. He trailed the remnants of Billy's gang to Stinking Springs, and before dawn on December 23, 1880, his posse surrounded the one-room stone house.

Charlie Bowdre was the first to rise. As he prepared to feed his horse, he was shot dead as he stood in the doorway.

After a day-long siege, Garrett convinces the others to surrender. After a quick trip to the Santa Fe jail (a marker exists at 208 West San Francisco Street, GPS 35.68755, -105.941), Billy was taken back to Lincoln.

After two years on the lam, The Kid had been captured, tried, and convicted of Sheriff Brady's murder. He was sentenced to hang at the Lincoln County Courthouse (GPS 33.493717, -105.390667), just paces from the scene of his worst crime in Lincoln.

The new courthouse was once the Murphy-Dolan Store, and the second-floor jail cell where Billy awaited his hanging had once been the bedroom of his old enemy, Lawrence Murphy. Sheriff Garrett assigned deputies Bob Olinger and James Bell to guard the elusive outlaw, who had escaped every time he'd ever been arrested. Billy was to remain shackled around the clock.

During the dinner hour on April 28, 1881—just two weeks before Billy's execution—Olinger escorted all the inmates but Billy across the street for supper at the Wortley

Hotel (GPS 33.493679, -105.389698). Billy asked Bell to take him to the outhouse behind the jail.

On their way back, the still-shackled Billy made his break. He grabbed a pistol from the jail's gun cabinet and shot Bell dead. (Jail visitors are always eager to see the purported bullet hole in the old stairwell where Billy killed Bell, but it probably wasn't made by Billy.)

Hearing the shots, Olinger ran back toward the jail but Billy blasted him with a double-barreled shotgun from a balcony and Olinger died in the yard.

With the help of a sympathizer, Billy hacked his shackles off, stole a horse, and fled into the twilight.

Robert Olinger (1841-1881) was buried in New Mexico's Old Fort Stanton Cemetery (now on private land at GPS 33.489996, -105.515913) His grave was unmarked and is now lost, but he is memorialized on Panel 13 (W-3) of the National Law Enforcement Officers Memorial in Washington DC (400 block of F Street NW, or GPS 38.89673, - 77.017564).

James W. Bell (1853-1881) was buried in Cedarvale Cemetery in White Oaks, New Mexico. His grave is in the southeastern corner

The spot where Billy the Kid killed Deputy J.W. Bell during his escape.

at GPS 33.74127, -105.74574. He is also memorialized beside Olinger on the National Law Enforcement Officers Memorial in Washington DC.

Two stones mark the sites of their deaths outside the Lincoln County Courthouse, now a museum.

THE END OF THE KID
Fort Sumner, New Mexico
The Maxwell house (long gone) was in the old Fort Sumner Officers Quarters, or GPS 34.40398, -104.20006.

For more than two months, Billy evaded capture, but Sheriff Pat Garrett didn't give up.

When Garrett heard a rumor that Billy's girlfriend, Paulita Maxwell, might be pregnant with the outlaw's child, he gathered a posse and rode to Fort Sumner, where The Kid and Garrett both had many friends. Garrett went straight to Pete Maxwell, one of those mutual friends and Paulita's brother.

Around midnight on July 14, 1881, while Garrett was in Maxwell's bedroom and his deputies sat at the far end of the Maxwell porch, The Kid unwittingly stumbled in.

Seeing the deputies on the porch, he drew his six-shooter and whispered in the dark to Maxwell, "Quien es?" (*Who is that?*) as he backed toward the door. Maxwell, in turn, whispered to Garrett, "El es" (*It's him*). Garrett fired twice, hitting Billy in the heart.

Billy the Kid was dead.

BILLY'S FUNERAL
Fort Sumner, New Mexico
The grave is in the Fort Sumner Cemetery, at GPS 34.40752, -104.193546.

After a coroner's inquest ruled Billy's killing was a justifiable homicide, Garrett permitted the outlaw's friends to wash and clothe his body for burial in the old post cemetery.

Paulita Maxwell later said she and several women took The Kid's corpse to a carpenter shop where they laid him on a wooden bench. She said they stuffed a rag in the bullet hole in his back to keep him from leaking, and placed lighted candles around him.

The next day, he was placed in a pine coffin and taken by wagon to the cemetery less than a half-mile away.

In his memoirs, Garrett wrote that Billy's exact age when he died was twenty-one years, seven months, and twenty-one days, but he might have been as young as nineteen. Historians believe Garrett preferred to think he'd killed an adult male rather than a teenager.

Billy the Kid's purported grave in Fort Sumner, but in reality nobody's exactly sure if that's where he lies.

William Henry McCarty, alias Billy the Kid, was laid between two old friends who also died as outlaws, Charlie Bowdre (1848-1880) and Tom O'Folliard (d. 1880).

A 1904 flood ravaged the cemetery, washing away headstones and graves. In 1932, a new headstone was placed on the approximate site of Billy's grave, but nobody's absolutely certain it's in the precise spot.

After Billy's tombstone was stolen in 1950 and 1981—and subsequently found—an iron cage was placed over the grave to thwart vandalism. In 2012, vandals again knocked over the 2,000-pound stone.

A replica grave exists in the nearby Billy the Kid Museum, 1601 East Sumner Avenue (GPS 34.466418, -104.229357).

But the next phase of Billy the Kid's legend was just starting.

DID THE KID SURVIVE?

Old West outlaws and their legends die hard. And some say Billy the Kid didn't die the way history said.

In all, some twenty-six men have claimed to be Billy the Kid, whose final escape was apparently his greatest. So if you've been to Billy the Kid's "official" grave in Fort Sumner, your graveyard tour isn't done.

In Hamilton, Texas, you can visit the grave of Ollie "Brushy Bill" Roberts (1858-1950), who claimed in his twilight years to be the genuine Billy the Kid. At least six books have been written about him, and lots of people are convinced Brushy Bill is the real Kid. Oakwood Cemetery is on the east side of US 281 just north of Hamilton, or GPS 31.71685, -98.11908.

When Brushy Bill's "true" identity was discovered in 1948, he claimed a look-alike friend was actually killed by

Sheriff Pat Garrett and that he embarked on an incredibly adventurous life as a Wild West Show performer, a Pinkerton agent, an aide to "Hanging Judge" Isaac Parker, a Rough Rider and a volunteer with Pancho Villa. In 1949, he attended a birthday party for his friend J. Frank Dalton, who claimed to be the real Jesse James. In 1950, Brushy Bill asked the New Mexico governor for a pardon, but his case was never heard. Brushy Bill died of a heart attack on a Hamilton street at age 90.

A New Mexico historian recently found a notation in a Roberts family Bible that suggests Brushy Bill was born too late to be Billy the Kid.

Unconvinced? Well, Brushy Bill has *two* museums dedicated to his life. Visit the Billy the Kid Memorial Museum at 211-C North Rice in Hamilton (GPS 31.70523, -98.12366). Owner Myrna Carpenter actually knew Brushy Bill, and among the period pieces she displays are a pair of his spurs and a leather holster. You may also visit the Billy the Kid Museum, 114 North Pecan Street in Hico, Texas (GPS: 31.98192, -98.03087).

Then there's John Miller (1850-1937), an ordinary fellow who claimed to be Henry McCarty.

Miller's proof? He had buck teeth, was a good shot, and got along well with shady folks. When he got married in Las Vegas, New Mexico, on August 14, 1881—just a month after his near-fatal encounter with Pat Garrett—his family said he wore a six-shooter and a bandage over a severe chest wound.

Miller died at the Arizona Pioneers Home in Prescott on March 14, 1937, and was buried in the home's cemetery (Row W, Grave 8 at GPS 34.563237, -112.486345). He was eighty-six.

In 2005, investigators exhumed Miller's bones for DNA to compare to blood from the carpenter's bench where Billy's corpse supposedly lay after the shooting (found on a Fort Sumner ranch). Efforts to exhume the bodies of Billy and his mother were thwarted. To date, no conclusive DNA test results have been made public. (Whether the real Billy's DNA is on the bench or in Miller's marrow, they won't match. But, hey, it's a great story.)

SHERIFF PAT GARRETT
Las Cruces, New Mexico
Masonic Cemetery is at 760 South Compress Road. Garrett's grave is in Section 7, Block 11, or GPS 32.30113, -106.78552.

Alabama-born Patrick Floyd Jarvis Garrett vaulted into Old West legend by killing Billy the Kid. He wrote a book about it, but some conspiracy theorists say it never happened, or at least not the way he said. In some fanciful alternative theories, Garrett helped his friend Billy fake his death or lied about killing somebody he mistook for Billy. Others think even Garrett was fooled by a lookalike while Billy lived on.

Pat Garrett

Garrett was only thirty-one at the time of Billy's supposed death, but he was suddenly a celebrity lawman across the nation. He served as sheriff in several New Mexico counties, dragging his big family from town to town. In 1896, he worked hard to find the killers of Albert Jennings Fountain and his eight-year-old son Henry, but his prime suspects were acquitted, and the case never solved.

He retired soon after and took a job as a US Customs inspector in 1901. But after a couple years, Garrett was out of work and back on his ranch near Las Cruces.

On March 1, 1908, while riding his buggy to Las Cruces, Garrett met one of his ranch's tenants, Wayne Brazel, near Alameda Arroyo.

The two men argued angrily about their lease as they rode toward town. When Garrett stopped his buggy to urinate, he was shot once in the back of the head and once in the belly. He died in the dirt at age fifty-seven.

Four days later, the six-foot-three Garrett was buried in a specially made coffin in Masonic Cemetery. Brazel surrendered himself and confessed to killing Garrett, but he was acquitted with the help of a corrupt lawyer named Albert B. Fall, later convicted in the notorious Teapot Dome scandal.

Many people believed a deeper, darker conspiracy killed Pat Garrett, engineered by Fall and a shady rancher named Oliver M. Lee, one of Garrett's

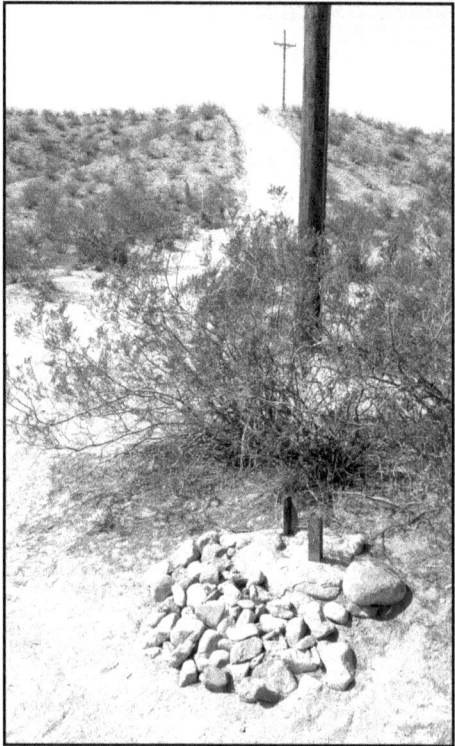

The remote spot near Las Cruces where Pat Garrett was murdered was marked in the 1930s by his son but is now threatened by development.

suspects in the Fountain disappearance.

Others blamed local powerbroker William Webb Cox (buried not far from Garrett at GPS 32.30039, -106.78411) or cowboy Carl Adamson. And many believe the famous Old West assassin "Killer" Jim Miller did the dirty deed.

Nonetheless, Garrett's killing remains an open question.

In the late 1930s, Garrett's son Jarvis marked the crime scene with a crude monument of concrete and rocks. It's still there in the scrub beside a narrow utility road (GPS 32.366203, -106.717152), about 1.2 miles south of a highway marker at the intersection of US 70 and South Jornada Road (GPS 32.379585, -106.730027). The wild area is surrounded by encroaching subdivisions and is difficult to find, but the City of Las Cruces has protected it as a park to preserve it from destruction.

Today, a 3,000-pound bronze monument to Garrett also exists behind the Chaves County Courthouse in Roswell (GPS 33.397059, -104.520953).

And pop culture has paid tribute to Garrett in dozens of films, where he has been portrayed by Wallace Beery (*Billy the Kid*, 1930), James Coburn (*Pat Garrett & Billy the Kid*, 1973), and John Wayne's son Patrick (*Young Guns*, 1988), among many others.

YOUNG GUNS, OLD FOES, LAST LOVE

▪ **Josiah Gordon "Doc" Scurlock** (1850-1929) studied medicine in Louisiana, but "Doc" wasn't a doctor. Instead, he was a vicious gunfighter until New Mexico Governor Lew Wallace — author of *Ben Hur*— pardoned all the Regulators (except The Kid). That's when Doc moved to Texas, where he gave away his guns, took a job with the highway department and allegedly wrote book reports for University of Texas students before dying of a heart attack at age seventy-nine. He's buried in the City Cemetery in Eastland, Texas (400 South Halbryan Street, or GPS 32.397783, -98.812533). In the 1988 film *Young Guns*, Scurlock was played by Kiefer Sutherland.

▪ Cousins **Frank and George Coe** survived the 19th century and after drifting around the West, returned to Lincoln County. Frank (1851-1931) was briefly detained for the murder of Buckshot Roberts but released. His final resting place is unknown. George (1856-1941) started a store and ranch. In 1934, he published his memoir *Frontier Fighter*. He died of natural causes at his ranch and is buried in the private Coe-Perry Family Cemetery (GPS 33.40780, -105.44690) near Glencoe, New Mexico.

▪ **Jose Chavez y Chavez** (1851-1924) was already a small-time criminal when he joined Billy's gang during the Lincoln County War. After Billy's death, he tried going straight, but failed. A multiple murderer, he was imprisoned for life until pardoned in 1909. He died of natural causes and is presumed buried in Milagro, New Mexico. In the 1988 movie *Young Guns*, he was portrayed by Lou Diamond Phillips.

▪ **Lawrence Murphy** (1831-1878) was one of the prime instigators of the Lincoln County War and arch-enemy of Billy's Regulators. A former Union officer in the Civil War, he was buried in the Santa Fe National Cemetery (Section C-499, GPS 35.695270, -105.948896) after he died of cancer at age forty-seven.

▪ **James Dolan** (1848-1898) was also a driving force behind the Lincoln County War on the opposite side of Billy's Regulators. He acquired John Tunstall's property, became a territorial senator, and died at age fifty. He's buried at the Fritz Cemetery in Lincoln (GPS 33.409419, -105.285846)

▪ **Lew Wallace** (1827-1905) might have reneged on his promise of amnesty for Billy the Kid, as the outlaw's supporters say, but in 2010 Governor Bill Richardson also rebuffed a pardon request because of "a lack of conclusiveness and the historical ambiguity." *Ben-Hur* author Wallace is buried at Oak Hill Cemetery in Crawfordsville, Indiana.

▪ **Joseph McCarty-Antrim** (c. 1862-1930) was Billy's only sibling but grew up without his brother's criminal tendencies. He was an itinerant bartender, cook and gambler who ended up penniless in Denver. He reportedly vowed to kill Pat Garrett on sight, but in 1882 he met Garrett in Colorado and they talked for two hours; afterward, Joe said he understood his brother's slaying better. When he died, nobody claimed his body so it was donated to the University of Colorado Medical School.

▪ **Paulita Maxwell Jaramillo** (1864-1929) told fond stories about Billy for the rest of her life. If she wasn't pregnant at the time of the outlaw's death, she was soon after. A son, Telesfor, was born in early 1882, and some say hebore a striking resemblance to Billy, but it will likely never be known if the child was Billy's—Telesfor died young. Paulita hastily married in the months after The Kid's death. She died at age sixty-five. The Abreu family marker in the Fort Sumner Cemetery carries Paulita's name, but it's not known if she's buried there.

FOR FURTHER READING

- *The West of Billy the Kid* by Frederick Nolan (1999, University of Oklahoma Press)
- *Billy the Kid: The Endless Ride*, by Michael Wallis (2008, WW Norton)
- *Billy the Kid: A Short and Violent Life*, by Robert Utley (1991, Bison Books)

Coming soon!

THE CRIME BUFF'S GUIDE TO

OUTLAW
ARIZONA

RON FRANSCELL

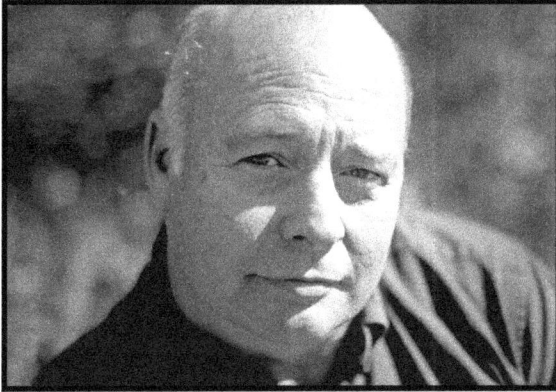

About the Author

Ron Franscell is a bestselling author and journalist whose atmospheric true crime/memoir **THE DARKEST NIGHT** was hailed as a direct descendant of Truman Capote's "In Cold Blood" and established him as one of the most provocative new voices in narrative nonfiction. Ron's lyrical but muscular prose has been compared to Robert Olen Butler, Cormac McCarthy and Charles Frazier, but his unique, evocative voice especially stands above others in true crime.

Franscell has written nine nonfiction books and three novels, including his bestselling literary debut **ANGEL FIRE**. He's also written three original screenplays, including the darkly funny western adventure **DEAD & GONE**, a recent quarterfinalist in the Academy Awards' prestigious Nicholl Screenwriting Fellowship.

Also by Ron Franscell

OTHER CRIME BUFF'S GUIDES

Crime Buff's Guide to Outlaw Arizona (2014)

Crime Buff's Guide to Outlaw Pennsylvania (2013)

Crime Buff's Guide to Outlaw Washington DC (2012)

Crime Buff's Guide to the Outlaw Rockies (2011)

Crime Buff's Guide to Outlaw Texas (2010)

NONFICTION

The Sourtoe Cocktail Club (2012)

Delivered from Evil (2011)

The Darkest Night (2008)

FICTION

Angel Fire (1998)

The Deadline (1999)

The Obituary (2003)

www.ingramcontent.com/pod-product-compliance
Lightning Source LLC
Chambersburg PA
CBHW060522030426
42337CB00015B/1969